For co-author, editorial, and corporation, association, university, or faith-based speaker requests, contact: Lady Mirage Agency, Inc. via:
www.LadyMirageGlobal.com

Scandals, Betrayers, & Liars:

Understanding How Deceivers Mean Business

A detailed story compiled over years of observation and documentation to recognize the red flags of dirty adult business acquaintances who play high school games, how to avoid them in the future to truly never again mix business with pleasure, and to warn others.

BY DR. KYLA LATRICE TENNIN, D.M., M.B.A., B.A.

Lady Mirage Publications, Inc.

New York Memphis Los Angeles Atlanta London Cape Town
Toronto Amsterdam Rio De Janeiro Singapore Japan

Copyright © 2019 by Kyla Latrice Tennin
The author is represented by Lady Mirage Literary Agency, Inc. All rights reserved. In accordance with the U.S. Copyright Act of 1976, the scanning, uploading, and electronic sharing of any part of this book without the permission of the publisher is unlawful piracy and theft of the author's intellectual property. If you would like to use material from the book, other than for review purposes, prior written permission must be obtained by contacting the publisher via email at LadyMirageLaw@gmail.com

Published March 2020 by:
Lady Mirage Global
c/o Lady Mirage Publications, Inc.
3724 Goodman Rd W, Unit 575
Horn Lake, MS 38637
United States of America
(Address will change in April 2020)

First Edition: July 09, 2019
Lady Mirage Publications, Inc. is an imprint and subsidiary of Lady Mirage Global, Inc. The Lady Mirage Publications, Inc. name and logo are trademarks of Lady Mirage Global, Inc.

Unless otherwise noted, all Scripture quotations are from the Everyday Life Bible Amplified Version of the Bible. Copyright © 2013 by Faith Words, Hachette Book Group publishers. Used by permission due to public domain access.
Cover photo provided by www.Google.com Public Domain Search

The publisher is not responsible for websites or their content that are not owned by the publisher.
Library of Congress Cataloging-in-Publication Data:
Print ISBN: 978-1-7348079-0-5; eISBN: 978-1-7348079-1-2
Tennin, Kyla Latrice.
Scandals, Betrayers, and Liars:
Understanding How Deceivers Mean Business
Pages cm; copyrighted materials.
1. Self-Help. 2. Business. 3. Leadership. 4. Christian
Library of Congress Control Number: 2019917854

Print Book Edition, License Note
This book is licensed for your personal enjoyment only. The book may be re-sold or given away to other people. Thank you for respecting the hard work of the author.

eBook Edition, License Note
This book is licensed for your personal enjoyment only. The book may not be re-sold, copied, or given away to other people, unless via a Family Group plan using a Family Manager a digital retailer offers. Otherwise, if you would like to share this book with another person, please purchase an additional copy for each recipient. Thank you for respecting the hard work of the author.

DEDICATION

I dedicated this book to men and women around the world who have been *Mirage's* in life; overlooked, betrayed, not good enough, slandered, lied on so others could steal from you or try to take your place, mistreated, misunderstood, misrepresented, pushed to the back of the line or the bottom of the pile even when you were the most talented in the room or company, and treated unfairly because of the dreams and talent God put in you. Additionally, I dedicate the book to men and women around the world who desire to *shift from being ordinary to extraordinary and* accomplishing what others said you would never be able to do again or never be able to do at all, whether personally or professionally.

ACKNOWLEDGMENTS

I want to *say thank you* to anyone who has ever betrayed, rejected, mistreated, teased, lied on, misused, cheated, or looked down upon me. You helped me become GREATER and launched me into my destiny.

Whenever someone throws bricks at you, use them to *build.* Build something greater, like brands, businesses, careers, your talent into your next opportunity, even your mansion, allowing great gain to derive from your pain. To exemplify, whenever you face opposition, *know* the opposition is an opportunity; a set-back for a set-up to secure victory, rejection for rewards, pain for gain, lack for prosperity to leave a legacy, misery for miracles, and put downs for promotion.

IT'S YOUR TIME…*to bounce back…and go up!*

What my enemies meant for evil, God meant for my good and used "it" to bless me. (Genesis 50:20 NKJV)

AUTHOR'S NOTE

Scandals, Betrayers, & Liars:
Understanding How Deceivers Mean Business
Copyright © 2019
Kyla Latrice Tennin
All Rights Reserved.

AFFIDAVIT

All content written herein is of opinion, from personal experience and of suggestion. Individual results based on recognizing *red flags* and applying *lessons learned* may vary from person to person and no results are guarantee.

ALL RIGHTS RESERVED

No portion of this publication may be reproduced, stored in any electronic system, or transmitted in any form by any means; electronic, mechanical, photocopy, recording or otherwise, without written permission from the author. Brief quotations may be used in literary reviews with the consent of the author and publisher.

ADDITIONAL CONTENT

The book has been made available on mobile devices via Adobe Digital Editions and DRM (Digital Rights Management). An auto table of contents (TOC) is inserted for readers who prefer reading the book on an electronic device or in Portable Document Format (PDF) to be able to click on a section title in the TOC and be taken directly to the corresponding section.

Scandals, Betrayers, & Liars: Understanding How Deceivers Mean Business
Table of Contents

DEDICATION 4
ACKNOWLEDGMENTS 5
AUTHOR'S NOTE 6
AFFIDAVIT 6
Table of Contents 7
PREFACE 11
    PART 1 16
    GETTING ACQUAINTED 16
CHAPTER ONE 17
How We Met 17
Sam, Tim, Michelle, and Michelle's Cousin 19
The Awards Show 22
    Online Advertisement 23
    Hotel Gossip, Contracts, & Hotel Room Dispute 25
    Hotel Photoshoot 29
    A Gentleman and Casino Strip Dinner 32
    The Rest of the Evening 35
SCRIPTURE REFERENCES 35
RED FLAGS 36
LESSONS LEARNED 36
CHAPTER KEY POINTS 37
CHAPTER TWO 38
Learning People's Behaviors 38
The Following Year Awards Show 40
    Dressing Room Discernment 43
Third Awards Show 46
  Sam's Behavior Before, During, and After the Event 48
SCRIPTURE REFERENCES 57
RED FLAGS 59
LESSONS LEARNED 59

CHAPTER KEY POINTS 60
   PART 2 61
   BETRAYAL AT ITS FINEST 61
CHAPTER THREE 62
Me, Me, Me 62
A Black History Month Event 65
A Community Event to Raise Awareness 71
Fashion Week Meeting and Advertisements Photoshoot. 73
A Business Training 75
Record Label Promotional Materials 78
Sam's Concert and Losing Invested Finances 80
SCRIPTURE REFERENCES 86
RED FLAGS 88
LESSONS LEARNED 89
CHAPTER KEY POINTS 90
CHAPTER FOUR 91
Deception and Mind Games 91
Michelle's Patterns, Character, and Reputation 94
   Our Company's Reputation 96
Michelle's New Love Interest 98
   I Talked Too Much, Too Soon, & Trusted Too Early ... 100
   Michelle and Confrontation 102
Nashville Event and Physical Touching 104
   Sam's Birthday's, Meetings, Studio Visits, & Being Out of Town 111
SCRIPTURE REFERENCES 115
RED FLAGS 116
LESSONS LEARNED 118
CHAPTER KEY POINTS 118
CHAPTER FIVE 120
Scandals and Perpetual Betrayals 120
Do You Have $200: A Luxury Vehicle 123
Higher Education and Nicknames 132

Money, Best Friends, and Loyalty Agreement 133
A Romantic Relationship? 136
   I've Always Been Interested in You; A Hidden
   Girlfriend 137
A Colleagues' Wedding and A Valentine's Day Scandal 137
   Facebook Friend Requests 144
SCRIPTURE REFERENCES 151
RED FLAGS 158
LESSONS LEARNED 159
CHAPTER KEY POINTS 163
     PART 3 165
     GODS MASTER PLAN 165
CHAPTER SIX 166
Repositioning and New Perspectives 166
The Holy Spirit and Documentation 170
   Nassau, Bahamas Trip and Jet Skiing 172
   Self-Led Revenge or God's Vengeance? 174
   Beef Up Security in Your Life and Organizations 188
   God-led Business Decisions 191
SCRIPTURE REFERENCES 192
RED FLAGS 194
LESSONS LEARNED 194
CHAPTER KEY POINTS 195
CHAPTER SEVEN 198
Treading Carefully 198
Ten Years of Periodic Observation 199
   Unknown Email Sender & Photographs 201
   Social Media Blocking 205
   How Deceivers Mean Business 207
   Michelle's Christian Ministry 209
   Wheat versus Tares 210
Birthing this Book and Warning You 212
Protecting Yourself, Reputation, Career, and Ventures .. 213

Blessings and Curses 217
Virgins Without Oil: Missed Opportunities, New Levels,
and Next Dimensions of Success 219
Restoration of Everything, and then Some 222
SCRIPTURE REFERENCES 224
RED FLAGS 227
LESSONS LEARNED 228
CHAPTER KEY POINTS 229
A QUICK PRAYER 231
AUTHOR BIOGRAPHY 233

PREFACE

This is a book that every leader of an organization must read! The audience for the book is individuals from a variety of professions, experiences, backgrounds, organizations, and levels of growth in life. So, some of the language applied in the book is to accommodate different readers and is therefore, balanced so distinct people, practitioners, leaders, and constituents can understand contexts described, what God has to say about what happened to you, within your organization, or with a business deal by describing one foundational scenario to you out of various scandals and betrayals I encountered. The language is also balanced so readers can comprehend recommendations I convey on how to *recognize and survive* scandals, betrayers, and liars, and what to do afterwards.

Sometimes liars are defined as people who are *too-faced* and betrayers as *back-stabbers*. Liars are most often referred to as gossipers, pretenders, *deceivers*, cheaters, exaggerators, and people who commit fraud[1]. A liar is also a counterfeit, defamer, and slanderer[2]. Both types of people are disloyal and operate in dishonesty, falsehood, immorality, and hidden agendas. Morality regards right versus wrong.

My calling as a leader of organizations, primitively, but also within societies and communities has afforded me the opportunity to work with professionally, mentor,

---

[1] Merriam-Webster, Inc. (2019). *Merriam-Webster dictionary app*. Retrieved from https://play.google.com/store/apps/details?id=com.merriamwebster

[2] Merriam-Webster, Inc. (2019). *Merriam-Webster dictionary app [thesaurus]*. Retrieved from https://play.google.com/store/apps/details?id=com.merriamwebster

advise, and volunteer with numerous businesses. Such appointments have allowed me to recognize with hands on experience and deep observation, complexities that hinder not only firms from growing, but leaders from progressing.

There are many professional reasons for lack of growth in a leader's career, yet there are also personal issues that spill over into the workplace, whether in a physical office, while traveling, or in the field. Meanwhile, individuals try to keep personal problems hidden from their profession, but the truth is personal problems are within some people's professions because of the individuals they encounter and must deal with along the way, like working with family members in a family business or with a best friend on a new venture. Comparably, problematic business acquaintances with character, integrity, personality, psychological, professional, behavioral, and social identity issues bring such issues into professional relationships and possible partnerships.

Nevertheless, this book is a text the devil did not want me to write because it exposes his characteristics of scandal, betrayal, and lying. The devil repeatedly used people to try to distract me from bringing the book to fruition, so I know the text is valuable and can help someone learn, grow, recover, and advance after a scandalous, betraying, or lying catastrophe. God represents love and many people pretend, mask, and falsify who they are by portraying themselves as being of The Christ, but operate in evil, inappropriate, and deceiving mannerisms. Sometimes it takes a while to identity such persons because they conceal true motives and agendas, yet actions reveal great details. Still, as you monitor people over time you will recognize patterns of obscurity, which were present in the individual all along. New leaders need to be taught how to see red flags people bring to a situation, but veteran leaders are expected to have had previous experience.

For veteran leaders this is not always the case and reading or hearing about distinct approaches people who engage in scandals, betrayals, and lies take on can prepare anyone for a blind-sided battle lying in wait ahead. Scandals, betrayals, and lies will come in life, disguised as offenses, tactics the devil and people use in attempt to hinder, stop, move, or hold you captive in a space or time. The Bible states, it is impossible for offenses, in some way to not meet a person at some point in their life (see Luke 17:1). However, the challenge is how will one respond, and will you see such negative activities as opportunities instead, stepping stones to you next levels and dimensions of success in your personal and professional life, guarding your dreams so you can always move forward no matter what?

Moreover, offenses also cause other problems in one's life, like anger, hostility, revengeful thoughts, bitterness, unforgiveness, immobile spiritual growth, and an invisible barrier between you and God. As a result, prayers go unanswered and blessings do not flow. Therefore, the book has two purposes and the first is to use the book as a tool to publicly discuss *some of the mistreatments* from one set of individuals I encountered, through scandals, betrayals, and lies, although I have faced betrayals from many people. God told me to write the book to publicly expose unfair situations and people who tried to hide or cover up with time, scandals, betrayals, and lies; people will try to hide wrongdoing to get away with what they are doing or did. Inclusive, I do not have a problem with people who participate or get caught up in a scandal, betrayal, lie, or who act inappropriately towards someone once or twice and repent, but when the wrongdoing repeatedly occurs beyond the second time and no genuine acknowledgement of the misconduct and attempt to alter actions, the individual, his or her practices, and acquaintances need to be appraised and brought out in the open. God agreed.

Mistreatment can become abuse after a period of time. For example, if a person plays mind games with someone, the individual engages in manipulation tactics, causing confusion within the person targeted or between a group of persons, which can be equivalent to mental abuse. Likewise, people can, attempt to, and will abuse your time, resources, money, love, friendship, company, association, and life if you let them, so don't.

Henceforward, I separated the book into three parts (getting acquainted, betrayal at its finest, and Gods master plan) accompanied by the events relevant to those parts that occurred with the acquaintances. In each chapter I delineated what the individuals did to me inappropriately, a few strategies of how I responded, what God says throughout scripture about each person's behaviors, lessons I learned from each component of the scandal and betrayal scenario discussed in the book, and key points of each chapter I want you to remember so you can overcome immorality, not be defeated or become stagnant, and succeed in business, your workplace, and/or life.

Essentially, each encounter I had with each individual lead up to one main plotted scandal and betrayal, a major betrayal on valentine's day in the year 2010. Still, I found out that God had a greater plan for my life and was *protecting me in affliction*, not only during the 2010 valentine's day misconduct, but with all of the scandals, betrayals, and being lied on I faced. Therefore, the second purpose of the book is to warn individuals in business about false persons, how to recognize and address such persons expeditiously using some, not all, of my strategies, like discernment, prayer, Wisdom (God), and Gods Word, to be able to avoid strife, court cases, business interruption, a tarnished reputation by not responding to scandals, betrayers, and lies in an ungodly fashion, to operate in excellence, and know what to do when calamity presents itself. As an illustration, two of my colleagues frequently say, stay focused on getting ahead instead of trying to get even and never engage in worthless warfare's. The advice is powerful, I recommend you apply it.

    Lastly, some of you might just be looking for a spiritual explanation to what happened to you when calamity arose. I supply some explanations in the book which I pray will help move you forward in life and business.

-Dr. Kyla L. Tennin, D.M., L.S.S.W.B., P.M.E.C., M.B.A, B.A.

PART 1

GETTING ACQUAINTED

CHAPTER ONE
How We Met

People come from various walks of life and are *influenced* by family members, upbringing or childhood, friends, business partners, colleagues, personal or academic experiences, cultural background language, and other extremities of external surroundings, like television, movies, and conversations with acquaintances. Conversations can either positive or negative. And the problem with extremities or limits is limits can hinder and greatly impact a person's growth, thinking, motives, goals, and responses to other people, places, and things.

Regarding surroundings, and this mind sound cliché, but do you remember the saying, birds in a feather flock together? Similarly, when I consider immediate and extended family members, high school friends and clicks, executives and close colleagues in c-suites, celebrities and reality television shows, yacht clubs, books clubs, fraternities and sororities, philanthropist circles, a variety of social contexts, and the like, you name it, each have something in common and is why they associate. The former can also be applicable to racial, ethnic, political, and gender groups. For instance, in elementary and high school, at lunch, I remember girls always formed friendships with girls the fastest before becoming friends with boys. And in the workplace, women formed friendships with other women and went out for coffee after work or for lunch during the work-day. Primitively, connections were formed because individuals shared common interests, values, or beliefs, whether professionally or personally.

The same is true for cultures and sub-cultures of communities and nations. Besides, values of cultures are impacted by environments and the culture or objectives of a business sets the identity for the enterprise. Too, I have read enough textbooks in academia to know culture can be comprised of different levels or comes in many forms, like group, national, and workplace culture. Yet, each form affects individuals and shapes people's and company's identities.

However, as a global leader, when I reflect on national cultures and governments in other countries, I think about practices in Eastern hemisphere organizations and societies versus Western hemisphere corporations and humanities. Culture influences what individuals internal and external to a business expect from the company and how they view the institutions leader or leaders. An example is in leadership. Leadership is viewed more seriously in Turkey, Asia, and North Korea than in the United States. Inappropriate leadership actions are classified and dealt with differently in the United States than in Eastern hemisphere organizations, whether a small business, small-medium-enterprise, or a large firm. What leaders who act badly in Eastern hemisphere nations are punished for, Western hemisphere leaders of entities sometimes get away with.

In Eastern hemisphere countries, the punishment for seemingly small bad behaviors leaders of companies commit is typically hard labor, numerous years in prison, or life in prison. A prime exemplification of this could be fraud, some sort of theft or embezzlement, corruption, bribery, contracts inflation via bribery, extortion, false statements, coercion, or perhaps attempting to get revenge on an employee, independent contractor, business partner, or colleague who did you wrong. I title getting revenge *retaliation* in some of my corporate presentations because retaliation can also occur against whistleblowers by leaders, other employees, or human resources personnel.

Revenge and retaliation are mainly the same and whenever you try to retaliate against someone wronged you, if a physical fight happens, assault charges could be filed, which is why I do not understand some reality television shows! Many are breeding grounds for strife. We will discuss more about this in chapter six within the self-lead revenge section and in chapter seven under the protecting yourself, reputation, career, and ventures section.

    For now, either way, bad behavior and connections or acquaintances can impact a leader's ability to lead in general, lead effectively, and lead with authority, initiating reputational issues. Leaders unexpected or expected inappropriate actions can negatively impact the identity of a business he or she owns or his or her employer. As a result, immoral actions possess the capability of threatening the identity of a firm, whether presently, within the short time to come, or sometime in the distant future. Each are things I had to *guard* since the first day I met Sam, Tim, and Michelle in person after I invited them to work with the entertainment arm of our conglomerate starting with an awards show, and had an encounter with Michelle's cousin via a scandal Michelle helped conspire against me in the year 2009 leading into February 2010.

Sam, Tim, Michelle, and Michelle's Cousin

    To begin with, names of the people conveyed throughout the book are labeled with pseudonyms for protection and to respect the individual's privacy and confidentiality. Sam went to high school with some of my relatives years ago because they lived near him and we are all originally from the same state. I did not attend high school with them nor in the state I was from because I moved around a little bit because my father was in the military, a Marine, who was an aircraft engineer/technician and he and my mother later divorced, and moved again, to different states. I met Sam in 2006 or 2007 via a historical social media website when researching independent (indie) recording artists, record labels, and the like to possibly work with when I moved to a city close to theirs.

Sam's company logo stated the business was about something along the lines of loyalty, respect, trust…and money. Therefore, I was interested in working with him because of the respect and loyalty, in which trust follows. Loyalty regards supporting other individuals and organizations and in several manners. When supporting other businesses, the mission, vision, and values of the company are supported.

Meanwhile, I resided in another state thousands of miles away from Sam and some of the individuals, venues, and events I was seeking to work with to expand the entertainment division of our *conglomerate corporation*. Some of the other divisions of the conglomerate are food & beverage, retail stores, commercial and residential properties, film and productions, sports, consumer products, and a leadership academy.

In 2006 and 2007 our main company was our *entertainment arm* of the business where we assisted other firms with producing award shows, fashion weeks, health and beauty expositions (expos), music videos, major motion pictures, and other major events for communities while dabbling into technology and licensing. At that time, we were operating in twenty-two states in the United States of America and greatly within the Mid-West, primarily Chicago, Minneapolis, Indiana, Wisconsin, and Kentucky. We worked in Kentucky for the Kentucky Derby annual horse racing and sporting events and fashion and ambiance events we produced with entertainment and publishing partners. Off and on I ventured out to Dallas and Houston Texas for business seminars, trainings, and mass workshops with other entrepreneurs and possibly new business ideas, but I was primitively focused on expanding the entertainment arm of our organization to Eastern, Western, and Southern states in the United States to solidify our conglomerate position in the industry, eliminate some states we worked in to restructure the entire company and begin concentrating on the geographic locations God ordained for us to work in, for robust impact and greater work results.

Reorganizing included moving our marketing office functions to New York, sports to Atlanta and Los Angeles, a second headquarters in London, and other tasks. I was inspired to expand our enterprise after having a conversation with a celebrity colleague who lives in Chicago about business ideas I had and where the original company of the conglomerate and the company name came from. Prior to the conglomerate, I worked in the financial services sector, working with and assisting commercial and non-commercial businesses, for example, salons and landscaping companies, automotive dealerships, clinics/hospitals, consumers, and investors with financial matters.

Nevertheless, after writing proposal and powerpoint presentations for an event and presenting our company and materials to various individuals and organizations in 2007 to secure new partnerships, our company landed a partnership with an annual awards show, hence, partnerships are also about teamwork and unity. So, after developing written content for our organization for the awards show, agendas, securing photographers for innumerable events and activities, and considering talent for the event, I eventually spoke with Sam and he agreed to have his record label and band attend the next awards show and be our guests among other labels, bands, and individuals. During this time, I also met Tim, Sam's brother, and Michelle through the awards show when considering presenting her with a contract as an independent contractor within one of our organizations and came to know about Michelle's twin sister. I never met Michelle's twin sister because she ended up moving to another state and would not be able

> "…with many opportunities in one event".

to attend the show, despite other individuals from many states attending the award show every year and working with our organization. Michelle also has a brother, who lived in another state and attended the awards show after speaking with me on the telephone on numerous occasions and learning about the production. I invited him.

The Awards Show

The award show I was preparing my organization for in 2008 took some time planning because the event was an annual production. Attire, transportation, lodging, order of trophies and talent, and the like needed to be sorted out, and in later years, working with sound, microphone checks, performing with celebrity recording artists and bands members of our entertainment division knew the words of their songs to, taking photographs on the red carpet, mingling with guests, selecting individuals to provide courtesy awards show entrance tickets to, and responding to the press with interview requests and requests to take our photographs all needed to be accounted for. Organization and administration skills are a key part of producing awards shows. For the awards show our entertainment division was preparing for we were fortunate to not have to assist with producing the entire show and focused largely on our own small events and agendas throughout the awards show week and securing fashion models necessary for innumerable productions that would occur before, during, and after the production and subsequent events throughout the year.

Online Advertisement
	To secure the fashion models for the annual awards show over the years, our entertainment division contacted talent within our database, but also secured talent through an advertisement from a talent database our firm was a member of. Additional talent was exclusively contacted we located on a public fashion forum, which Michelle was located on and seemed to be reputable at the time and after speaking with her on the telephone on several occasions I learned she was in college, studying marketing. Michelle responded and stated she was interested and would be available to work with us and mentioned, later, her brother was a recording artist, the same brother I previously mentioned I had a conversation with and eventually invited to the event.
	The purpose of exercising the public forum to secure a few fashion talents from was to provide people who have not had many opportunities in the industry with many opportunities in one event. God created me with a conglomerate *mindset* and purpose to provide one-stop-shop products and services to businesses and consumers. For example, the planned awards show festivities would provide opportunities for exposure, networking, a chance to attend industry meet and greets, workshops and

seminars to learn about the business and high-ranking individuals in the industry, and obtain contact information for production houses, distributors, brands, disc jockeys, licensing companies, print publications, publishers, retail stores, radio stations program directors and managers, and the like.

    Our entertainment arm was also seeking to present talent with contracts, as independent contractors, for our developing fashion agency which later transitioned into a full-service creative agency with a talent board and later into an advertising and marketing firm for advertising, advertising related services. To be vague, our advertising services are for in-store, point-of-sale, digital technology, media buying and representation, behavioral and experiential (quantitative, qualitative, and mixed methods) research, consulting, and global market research while retaining our talent board. Michelle was being considered for a contract, but I was skeptical about her after noticing her behavior in the lobby of the casino hotel the awards show production company booked us to stay at for the week.

    Invitations sent to talent to attend the award show was for working and professional purposes to advance careers, ideas, and ventures, as a stepping-stone, not for gossip, hearsay, or connecting with the opposite sex to engage in a romantic relationship. However, I did not explicate such information clearly and concisely to attendees through email, telephone, and other written correspondence, nor in-person when we met. I did convey the information about attending the event for professional purposes and we were all there to work. Professionalism, which exudes ethics, is about earning the trust of people you work with, setting good examples, inspiring others by doing what is right, and encouraging and showing others how to be professional through development. In our case, talent working for us for distinct events were expected to be and model professionalism with their character, integrity, demeanor, and interaction with other attendees and event staff.

Nowadays, for new hires who are full-time employees (FTEs) with a new hire card on record at a state development authority, organization officials can present personnel with employee handbooks, responsible business, codes of ethics, privacy and solicitation, conflicts of interest and outside activities, and electronic communications and social media guidance policies, to name a few, to read and sign. Nothing seems to be in place for independent contractors and should be researched, developed, and tested for quality assurance for legal applicability to a corporation. Such documents would also be applicable for conglomerates with divisions or subsidiaries, whether wholly owned or not, that work with independent contractors by some form of written agreement, to hold contractors accountable for any negative outcomes or breaches so retainers take work seriously. And if necessary, to award monetary compensation for any castigatory damages done to the reputation of the business or loss of clients, connections, or partnerships, if applicable.

Hotel Gossip, Contracts, & Hotel Room Dispute

The casino hotel the production company selected for all staff to reside in was well chosen. Since our talent and guests were arriving from several different cities and states within the United States I asked everyone to meet at the hotel listed on our firm's itinerary and schedule of events that was supplementary to the schedule of events for the week for the awards show production. The *time* of

Scandals, Betrayers, & Liars | 26

each activity and event for our firm and for the award show was listed on the schedules. When I arrived at the hotel, each of the fashion models booked for the event were in the hotel lobby waiting for me, except one or two. Recording artists, their labels, and managers trickled in as we went about the afternoon and evening. Sam's label and band arrived later in the evening and I noticed, over time, they were late to everything afterwards too.

Upon arriving at the hotel as I began checking into our rooms I realized we were missing a hotel room under our institution's name, so I called my colleague at the production organization on his mobile phone and he came right over to the hotel's front desk to meet me there and begin resolving the issue. Getting everything resolved took some time, but not too long. As I was doing this, I said hello, waved to the models from a distance, went to greet them, and then went back over to the front desk. With getting the rooming situation taken care of through speaking with the front desk clerk and being attentive to the talent, I started noticing the look on some of their faces.

> "...spoke with her brother on the phone".

To see if I was discerning gossip was taking place I continued working with the clerk while observing the talent out of the corner of my eye, but without turning my head so they would not know I was observing. I did recognize Michelle speaking to one of the talents and smiling and then to another. As time progressed, some of the models began folding their arms as we waited for the reservations to be amended and the additional room paid for by the production company. I wondered what the conversations were about, but people know when someone is talking about them, particularly in a negative way by observing demeanor or body language, non-verbal behaviors, eye cues, and facial expressions. However, I did not want to pass judgement or think the worst about someone too soon because it was too early to determine the type of people our organization was about to work with and monitoring some of them over time was needed.

Based on the relatively low spoken conversations between the models in the hotel lobby, I decided to monitor the talents who talked the most. In advance, before arriving at the hotel I prepared company folders for each fashion model. All folders contained a company application to complete to work with the firm for the week and others included additional information, like a contract to continue working with the entertainment division over a certain amount of time. I did not give Michelle a contract.

While in our primary hotel room, I called a meeting among fashion models to discuss the content of their folders and met with some of them individually. I also discussed the awards show event and the week of activities with them in detail. Meanwhile, a hotel room dispute was brewing and was not related to the additional room that was missing from our original reservation. The hotel room dispute began after our meetings within our primary hotel room. We had some down time before the next item on our schedule, which was the hotel photoshoot.

During our down time, Michelle spoke with her brother on the phone, which if I recall correctly is her half-brother, and advised him about the events and her being at the hotel. I am not sure if he made a reservation at the hotel or for another place to stay for the evening or week prior to coming into the state for the show, but the dispute began. Likewise, I have a problem with being too nice. When someone does not have a place to stay during company productions, I always seek to see if spare, paid for, hotel rooms exist, and/or if more people can be compiled into one room. I did this for Michelle's brother after finding out he did not have a hotel room reserved for the event, giving him one of our rooms. Michelle decided to stay with him that evening too, *with his girlfriend,* which I later found out from Michelle he brought; I believe Michelle told her brother our company would pay for his hotel room and without initially stating he was bringing his girlfriend.

    Conclusively, I believe Michelle and her brother discussed obtaining a room from me or planning how he could receive assistance with a place to sleep for the night or however long our company was planning on being at the event. I also believe Michelle was the main person behind taking advantage of my kindness to secure her brother a room based on another incident that occurred the following year when our firm worked with the same production company for a summer event in Nashville, an event Michelle could not attend, but spoke with me on the phone frequently as I was driving to the event. A slight argument happened between Michelle and I, Michelle's brother and I, and then between Michelle and I again, and is discoursed in chapter four. I had separate conversations with Michelle and her brother while driving, but should have discussed what we were discussing as a three-way conference call while not driving, but most significantly, should have not been speaking with Michelle's brother at all.

Hotel Photoshoot

Next, we were preparing for a photoshoot with a photographer, so the talent could receive individual photographs for their books (portfolios) to use to submit themselves for work for future industry opportunities. I also provided the ability to take photographs with some of the guests, labels, and recording artists our company invited and with other fashion models, for fun, and to begin bonding with one another.

The hotel photoshoot began with different recording artists and labels, prior to Sam's label arriving. Some of the labels and artists also owned retail clothing stores and music record stores. Other labels and recording artists whom did not own such ventures at the time, do today. As we worked with the first set of fashion models and recording artists, photographs went well until one fashion model revealed in her facial expressions she was unhappy about some parts of the shoot. This went on for a short period of time until I stopped the photoshoot after shooting several scenes to inquire about the situation. I initially did not want to intervene in the photographer's work, but found out the issue was one talent was upset about another talent taking more photos than her. The dilemma was petty, quickly resolved, and we moved on. From that point on I began supervising the photoshoot more closely and providing detailed creative direction, direction that would be best for future assignments in the industry for each participant.

Towards the beginning of the evening Sam and his record label arrived at the hotel. Sam was the chief executive officer (CEO) of his record label. As the photoshoot was taking place, Sam and his record label associates walked in and I saw him and immediately knew who they were and went to greet them. I advised them that the photoshoot was currently taking place and next on the schedule was his labels and bands slot to be photographed with the fashion models and Sam agreed. Prior to Sam's scheduled slot, hotel guests, individuals from our organization, and attendees of the awards show mingled in the hotel lobby, lounge, seating areas, and bar.

Right after his arrival, being greeted by me, and since he was waiting to be photographed, he wanted an alcoholic drink and I advised him the hotel had a bar and in which direction. He went over to the bar to purchase a drink and I followed him as my guest to ensure he found the bar. Sam purchase a brown alcoholic drink and we briefly chatted and laughed although I do not remember what the conversation was about. Yet, within seconds he asked me if I wanted a sip of his drink and I stated no, which was appropriate since I was working and do not drink. However, I have had a sip of three alcoholic drinks in my life and none of them were with Sam.

I have never been a drinker of alcohol because I was pre-medicine in undergraduate in college, love water more than alcoholic beverages, and saw the negative health and fatal impact alcoholic drinks had on the maternal and paternal side of my family. My father was one of the individuals who was fatally impacted by alcoholic drinks; after drinking so much he soon became an alcoholic, had behavioral and life coping issues, was abusive towards people, crashed automobiles, got into physical fights, and more, but I still loved him deeply. His alcoholism was a spiritual issue and did not end well the last 13 hours of his life in 2015. His organs began to fail, he blead out of his stomach *and* mouth, could not urinate himself, and began having brain issues, but still knew my voice and cried in his final hours trying desperately to lift himself out of his hospital bed. Who does such a thing when deeply wounded? My dad!

    My dad's behavior was typical since he had been hospitalized numerous times for the same alcoholic problem, blown up by bombs when serving in the military, and walking away from crashed automobiles. He loved Chevrolet Camaro cars, which could be the reason for my interest in sports and cars. Moreover, I disliked alcoholic drinks because of the impact I saw it had on my extended family members who drank with their children. And at the time Sam offered me a drink I was having a few health issues, which I later found out were spiritual problems causing natural health dilemmas.

    Nevertheless, after Sam purchased his drink Sam and I headed over to the area of the hotel where his record label's part of the photoshoot was starting and additional fashion models of our arrived for the awards show. Michelle watched Sam all night and seemed to be interested in him. So, I mentioned to her how handsome Sam was and she agreed, with high interest. I also discerned her high interest in wanting to take photographs with him and I did not mind, it was a photoshoot for our talent and invited guests. Yet, her interest was unusual, and I sensed a deep urgency I could not shake in my spirit, but brushed off the encounter and decided to not think about it anymore to remain professional.

    One thing I did notice in Sam and his associates photo session was he carried his alcoholic drink with him. Although he placed his cup on the ground when taking photographs, he sipped his drink when not being photographed. I do not recall him ever asking if it was okay to bring his beverage with him around like he proceeded to do because it would look inappropriate. Still, I never said anything about it, but should have to be proficient and protect the image of our company and myself, setting the tone for my personal and professional expectations. No one else at the photoshoot carried any kind of beverage around, neither did Sam's label mates.

As the evening advanced photoshoot time slots for members of other record labels and independent recording artists arose and were completed. Michelle participated and changed her demeanor over the evening to being more professional as artists were photographed with her. We finalized the photoshoot with group photographs of record labels, independent recording artists, fashion models, award show attendees, and I to signify we had a great time and wanted to remember the occasion.

A Gentleman and Casino Strip Dinner

The photoshoot ended well, dinner time was approaching, and as everyone prepared to retreat to the place's they reserved to rest at for the night attendees began advising me of their plans for the evening. Some of the attendees and recording artists were from in-state, the state of where the awards show was being hosted that year and told me they were driving home for the night, a one to two-hour drive and would return the next day while other artists and labels were staying at nearby hotels. I asked Sam where members of his label were staying for the night and what plans they had for the rest of the evening. Sam advised they were staying with a friend who lived about 45 minutes away and planned to drive the casino strip highway to look for a restaurant to order food. I stated the models and myself had not had dinner and asked if we could tag along (without thinking anything out of the ordinary would happen by just going to dinner), ride with his label in their vehicles, and Sam stated we could. So, I informed the models, told them they were welcome to change clothing and we would be leaving the hotel to go to dinner in a few moments.

Everyone agreed to attend and went to their respective hotel rooms to change and prepare for the night. As everyone said their goodbyes to one another, Sam and his label mates went to sight see the hotel and its amenities while the models and I went to change clothing. After the models finished changing, one by one and some together, they walked to the hotel elevators to head downstairs to the hotel lobby to wait for everyone else. I was one of the last persons to change clothing along with a couple of models, so we left the hotel room, some of Sam's label mates met us, and we rode the elevator together down to the lobby.

When we approached the lobby, Sam was waiting and smiling, and everyone began heading to the vehicles in the parking lot. I walked towards Sam and started smiling as well although I did not know what was so funny. As I approached Sam, he grabbed my arm and locked his arm in with mine, in a fashion to pretend like we were dating, a couple, and jokingly stated so aloud, but not disruptively. It did not bother me because we were just having fun.

The models, Sam, and I walked to one of Sam's record label trucks and we all decided to ride with Sam while his label mates rode in the other record label vehicle. Everyone was walking ahead of Sam and I out of the hotel and mid-way in between the entrance of the hotel and Sam's vehicle Sam told me it was cold outside, took off his jacket, and placed it around me to ensure I stayed warm. I was wearing a short-sleeved shirt, jeans, and open toe stilettos. I was a little cold, but not excessively, yet thanked Sam for the jacket and he smiled; I thought the jacket approach was very gentleman of Sam.

As the models approached Sam's car, he auto unlocked the vehicle, so the models would know which vehicle was his. When Sam and I got to his truck models were already getting into various areas of the truck and closing doors. I assumed everyone had gotten into different back seat areas of the vehicle until Sam opened his door to the front driver seat and I opened the passenger side door (Sam did not) to the other front seat and Michelle was sitting there getting ready to get settled in, to sit next to Sam. I laughed slightly and asked her what she was doing and to get in the back. She looked at me embarrassingly, gathered her things, and got out of the passenger seat and into the back of the vehicle with the rest of the models. I got into the front passenger seat and Sam smile, grabbed my left hand to rub it, started the engine, and bagged out to head to the casino strip with everyone else.

> "...seat and Michelle was sitting there"...

When Sam grabbed my hand, I politely snatched it back because I was shy, to be professional, and because I had never experienced something like that while working. I also decided to start a conversation about where everyone wanted to eat to change the mood.

As we were driving and deciding on a place to eat, Michelle rested the elbow of her arm on the divider between the two front seats and leaned in. I was checking text messages on my mobile phone and noticed an ex-boyfriend of mine was texting me excessively and had called a few times. He knew the awards show event was that weekend because he always called and texted excessively, and I advised him at one point that one of our organizations would be working at the show that week.

Nonetheless, he was texting me about starting our relationship again. Michelle kept looking at me as if she wanted to know what was going on, so I laughingly showed her the text message and she slightly laughed, but had a different agenda. Sam slightly looked at me, but kept driving and throughout that time Michelle kept an eye on Sam and me both.

The Rest of the Evening

Dinner for the evening was a chicken-based restaurant where people purchased food to go, but I decided not to eat because I was not hungry, focused on work, and reflected on the first part of the day and what I had to do the next day. The events for the first day of our organization's activities, aside from award show week activities were interesting. Many red flags surfaced throughout the day and evening I chose to ignore although I discerned and saw them with my own two eyes. Still, I wanted to enjoy the week, keep the peace, and be drama free although I did not intend on letting anyone *directly* take advantage of me.

SCRIPTURE REFERENCES

Biblical scriptures always help to put people, places, and things into perspective. Following, are scripture references, red flags, and lessons I learned as I reflected on what took place with people I met in chapter one:

- To practice integrity and steer clear of individuals who have a negative motive before or after meeting you, keep Psalm 26:5 in your heart, which states "do not associate with nor sit with false or *dishonest* people; do not fellowship with *pretenders* or opponents. "I hate the company of evildoers and will not sit with the *wicked*".

Opponents in the Bible refers to adversaries. Adversaries are enemies. Too, a person can start out being a nice person, but jealousy or deep evil intentions within them can arise to cause the person to eventually become an adversary. Throughout life, you must *watch over and guard* your own life, family, organizations, income, and destiny while also depending on God for direction, regularly.
- Regarding integrity and me being too nice, I always remember Matthew 5:41 that conveys "and if anyone forces you to go one mile, go with him two [miles]". Seek to follow a more excellent way even when no one is watching you.

RED FLAGS
- I had continuous imperceptible, faint, subtle problems with Michelle since the day I met her in the hotel lobby. She did a lot of talking about people, frequently watched people and places, and schemed a lot.
- People's present character, behaviors, and professionalism reveal details about how their acquaintance with you will be in the future.

LESSONS LEARNED
- Immediately remove problematic people from your personal and professional life. Otherwise, in the end, a connection or acquaintance with the person can prove to be catastrophic if they remain in your life or organization.
- Collaborating with people you have problems with can be beneficial, to learn what you will and will not tolerate and is sometimes necessary to get work done. However, focus on creating a broad and strategic network of key stakeholders who are genuinely

interested in positively promoting your organization and career, with reciprocity.
- The individual who is problematic can tell, is telling, or already told internal and external constituents of a firm inaccurate information about the business or the leaders of the entity. This can be discerned through observation of the problematic persons conversations (gossip) at company events.
- Allowing non-trustworthy and disloyal people to remain in your life or organization is breeding ground for future organizational and individual reputational damages. Constituents will have to conduct their own research to identify if inappropriate people's testimony of who you are or what your organization is about converges or diverges with what disloyal people said.
- Do not involve your personal life into your business matters. For example, never share details about your personal life with someone who is subordinate to you or *works for you* in your organization, too early.

CHAPTER KEY POINTS

- Whenever a person enters your life and you did not have continuous problems before meeting them, it is highly likely the new person is the one creating the problems, many times behind the scenes, while also claiming they are not doing anything.
- An individual may be beautiful or handsome on the outside, but if personality, behavioral, or verbal communication issues are present, the complexities stem from a person's internal being and will began to reflect on the outside. Communication is a skill and being able to effectively communicate with people is need for an association to be fruitful. Authentic open communication builds trust, not gossip.

CHAPTER TWO
Learning People's Behaviors

In practice, ethical leaders are equivalent with authentic leaders. Ethical leaders are authentic and show passion about their organizations, daily practice corporate values in their workplaces through their actions, and strive to create long-term relationships with stakeholders of the company and personnel. Authentic leaders have strong core values they implement into business practices, are committed to their entities, and are also known for not mimicking other leaders, but do regularly observe other leader's behaviors. The purpose of the observation is to learn what to do and what not to do.

As I consider what not to do, I think about leaders, who in a roundabout way, convey they are authentic or ethical, but their actions person tell something different. Their actions are hypocritical. Hypocrisy can occur in individual's professional and personal life and associations, which I have witnessed with several people. For some, personal life hypocrisy eventually spilled over into hypocrisy within professional work.

Moreover, for ethics, authenticity, and hypocrisy, consider a television or radio advertisement about new car promotions at a car dealership. If the advertisement does not exist when you arrive at the car dealership, the promotion could be considered a false advertisement that was harnessed to lure customers in the doors as an attempt to increase sales. Another example of hypocrisy could be an organization's logo implies the entity is about ethics and values by using the words *respect*, integrity, professionalism, *trust*, honesty, or *loyalty* and the leaders of the company behave contrarily. And for public companies listed on stock exchanges, company stocks or market valuation, particularly long-market valuation, is influenced positively if employees and executives of institutions behave appropriately. Behaving appropriately reveals a person's commitment to a business, workplace, connection, or profession.

As I mentioned in chapter one, Sam's company logo stated something along the lines of his record label was about loyalty, respect, and trust. I also discoursed and reiterated similar company values to individuals at my organization and our entertainment arm because the values are linked to our company name. Michelle was aware of this, which I discuss more later in chapter four regarding our company's reputation.

Nevertheless, ethics, authenticity, values, and morality (moral standards) are linked. Behaviors people display usually derive from moral standards and actions and moral standards affect the well-being of other individuals, whether within the workplace, a friendship, or some other acquaintance. Similarly, in my opinion, leaders who are ethical and authentic are more concerned about portraying the correct moral standards and how the standards will impact others than the leader's self-interest, which is a focus on *personal gain* instead of *shared interest*. When people are focused on personal gain, they are only interested in what you can do for them instead of what they can do for you or your company, reciprocally.

Over the years I have learned about people's moral standards, values, and self-interests by having a conversation with them, observation, and discernment. Discernment comes from God and needs to be developed, but to the modern-day person, discernment is typically referred to as a feeling someone gets in their *stomach* or *gut* (a gut feeling) about a person, place, or thing. Southerner's call discernment a right mind and use the statement "I should have followed my right mind". God frequently connects discernment with peace. If you do not feel at peace about someone, some thing, or some place, you are probably right and are *sensing* something important. Each of the feelings I just described are what I felt about Michelle at the following year awards show and about Sam after witnessing some of his behaviors.

The Following Year Awards Show
The color scheme of the following year awards show was schedule to be gold and black and expansively larger than awards show's in the previous years based on the number of tickets sold each year. Our company attire for the event was gold and black too. Equally, the number of attendees grew each year because the show was advancing in age and promotion. Each year, our entertainment division helped with spreading the word about the event to individuals and companies who had never attended. I also invited attendees our firm worked with from the prior year awards show to the following year awards show, like record labels, fashion models, independent artists, radio stations, and the like. Sam's record label, his label mates, and Michelle were some of those people.

Since I was very interested in individuals attending the awards show who did not have a great deal of former exposure to reputable people, radio stations, companies, and brands, print publication publishers, and the like, I invited numerous people. Some of the individuals I invited were record labels I was familiar with and colleagues whom I knew from past states our entity worked in who were presently living in the state the awards show was being held in.

Like the past awards show, the production company supplied me with free tickets to give out to people and groups I selected. Sam's label and label mates were some of those individuals to provide them with exposure. If Sam and his label did not arrive on time I planned to give their tickets and any other remaining tickets away to other labels, recording artists, and individuals I invited. Sam and his label mates were late and always late to every event and company function afterwards, including a subsequent awards show, which was our third year working with the production house. Sam nor Michelle attended the show the fourth year, but Michelle's brother kept attending events.

  Nevertheless, even though many attendees were present at the awards show, only people with tickets to the show were allowed into the venue. Yet, some individuals without tickets remained outside of the venue to mingle with similar guests and watch the awards show when people went in and out to use restrooms. As the door to the awards show opened and closed, persons standing outside of the entrance could see inside. I am not sure if this is what Sam and his label mates were doing, but they were still at the event when the awards show as over.

  Furthermore, well into the evening I saw Michelle quickly chatting with Sam and I seemingly gathered from the look on their faces she asked him for his contact information, he agreed, and the conversation quickly ended. The exchange of contact information could have or could have not taken place, but at the time I know Sam did not have any way of contacting her via any social media (social media that exists today did not exist then) and Michelle advised me during some of the betrayal incidents later down the road that her and Sam 'just kept in touch'. My question is for what? To book you for work, so you could provide your brother with his information to work on a project together or to get signed, or for your own personal agenda, even after I previously told you to remove yourself from the front seat of his vehicle and to get into the back?

Henceforward, some of the fashion models and I walked over to Sam and Michelle to begin discussing the rest of the evening. Everyone decided they would be heading home since events for the week were winding down and the awards show was completed. In the middle of the conversations I saw some of Sam's label mates walking to towards exits to possibly locate vehicles they drove in within the parking lot. Next, Sam just walked off during the conversations. As a result, the rest of us casually ended our discussions and decided to leave for the evening except a few of our talent who decided to take the remainder of their conversations to a bar although they did not drink alcoholic beverages. Entertainment industry leaders they were interested in connecting with business wise did.

I followed our talent in the direction they were headed in because the bar was near the parking lot where I parked. Sam was headed in that direction as well and must have parked nearby. Yet, Sam was walking too far ahead of me for me to catch up with him, so I called him on his cell phone to see why he just walked off and to ask him about his plans for the evening, thinking perhaps he would be interested in some of the industry conversations others were getting ready to engage in.

Sam did not answer his phone although I had just saw him seconds early. I dialed a second time and there was no answer. The issue with Sam and his label being late and me giving away the remainder of the awards show tickets could have been the problem and was a thought that crossed my mind. If the issue was the tickets, then surely a mature adult would communicate the problem. Then I thought the communication probably could not happen since I would have likely brought up his label being late to the event. Still, walking off when someone is speaking, but the exchange of contact information and a conversation with a talent *who I invited* to an event and was working for our organization for the evening was inappropriate and a red flag about Sam I later ignored, again, and should not have.

Dressing Room Discernment
     Discernment assists people with knowing the real or exact nature of individuals they deal with, whether evil or good; discernment helps people realize the true nature of a circumstance, message, conversation, and/or the real motive behind an individual. Someone can appear to be good or look good on the outside, for example, dressed a certain way, but discernment will cause a person dealing with the nicely dressed person to internally perceive something is not right about the presentable individual. Discernment or an uneasy feeling about a person is how God warns His children about a person's true intentions, which are evil. Whenever a person displays a good attitude, but has evil intentions or wicked thoughts, they are likely deceptive, use the good attitude to deceive, yet are planning or will at some point, attempt to destroy, hinder, or block someone or something. Wicked people who engage in such treason are usually interested in deceiving and demolishing to gain something or someone they want for themselves, or simply to stop your advancement.
     Within other betrayals, scandals, lies, and manipulated situations people pre-meditated and then tried to carry out against me, God had the situation work in my favor, to profit me spiritually, naturally, and

financially. Similarly, individuals who plotted the bad behavior were jealous of me; jealously was the root of their actions. Something is always at the root and individuals want you removed so they can gain access to or continue pursuing something or someone they want to pursue. Are you following what I am saying?

To paint a picture, lying, manipulation, and deceiving to carry out an evil plan does not only occur among *high school teenage girls* to steal someone's best friend or boyfriend, the football jockey or basketball star, but also in corporations. Some of my business colleagues faced such opposition within start-up companies and contractual agreements with like-minded institutions and individuals, only to find out they were being manipulated and used to advance a company or an executive's agenda and were planned to be cut out of a deal via written paperwork once the vindictive executive achieved what he or she wanted. For instance, removed from a career position, board of directors, or company entirely. Some of the malicious executives even lied on other executives about not completing certain work to prominent company leaders who were decision makers so the removal of the vulnerable or blind-sided executive could be successful.

Lastly, women adult betrayers and liars who plan high school teenager scandals to secure a man usually do not work alone and enlist other people to help them, which is cowardly, petty. Such cowardly or petty teenager moves to gain something unjustly have always been what I call *desperation moves*; individuals who engage in such scandals and betrayals are desperate to me. I would even go as far to say the teenage scandal is not of a 17 or 18-year-old high-schooler, but of someone who *acts* age 14 or 15 when they recruit other people to assist them.

A similar scenario can apply to adults at different ages. To demonstrate, I have seen people who are nearing age 60 act 20 by using manipulation of mind games, deceit, and scandal to steal from various individuals financially and materialistically and laughed about the schemes thinking the sins would not be realized and judgement from God will not occur. However, discernment always reveals who's who and evil people will always be held accountable for their actions, whether now or at the end of this age (see to Revelation 20: 11-15).

Hence, discernment kicked in while I was in the dressing room preparing for the awards show for the following year. For the dressing rooms, event attendees with our organization made the two large adjoined dressing rooms situation work by making mini dressing rooms out of different spaces within the space we were in. The environment was family friendly and respect filled the atmosphere, until I looked in my dressing room mirror to notice Michelle coming in to go to her section of the dressing room to prepare for the evening events. After getting dressed, I walked into Michelle's area to observe another talent assisting her with her dress. While assisting Michelle, Michelle was talking with the model, lowly. Usually when people talk low they are stating something they do not want someone else to hear, and in this case, gossip could have been occurring.

> "...watching Michelle's body language..."

The energy Michelle exuded was not welcoming and was something I brushed off, again, but housed in my spirit to critically observe over the evening. I also began watching Michelle's body language during the whispered conversation. Her body language spoke volumes of gossip and was something I did not like, but I decided to get on with the show. Still, the negative verbal and body language cues did not cease, including skeptical eye movements, but Michelle pretended to act cordial although I knew the individual I was dealing with was not pleasant and red flags kept adding up. Her cordial actions to anyone with high discernment, were counterfeit.

Third Awards Show

For our third year working with awards show, the event was held in the same state, but at a different casino. The purpose of the event being at the casinos was for space, the several rooms the venue had that could accommodate industry workshops, additional events, and the like, according to what the production company wanted. Our talent, persons affiliated with our organization, nor I are gamblers. Furthermore, venue amenities were also a plus for guests and attendees who were interested. For our third year working with the production administration and awards show, which is the foundation of this book to illustrate scandal, betrayal, and liars, Michelle did not attend.

Michelle could not attend due to her job as a server at a restaurant in her state. She had to work, did not have a babysitter, lacked reliable transportation, and was dealing with her ex-husband, the father of her child. As Michelle told me on the telephone about each of the four major reasons for her not being able to attend the third-year awards show, which I felt sorry for her, our conversation quickly turned into a friendship conversation and she told me about a new guy she met (e.g. a love interest) and possibly wanted to date, but was taking things slow since was working on being a Christian.

Taking things slow meant she did not want to move the relationship along too fast because sexual intercourse could result, and she did not want to appear a certain way to the guy, especially with just meeting him. I assumed she was talking about appear as a whore for sleeping with a man too soon.

For the third awards show, all of our staff and talent who attended the show wore the same color attire, as we do for every event, to be recognizable, and align with the colors of the event. So, for the third show I had everyone wear red attire. I was told by production company owner the third-year event was planned to be slightly smaller than the previous based on ticket sales, but was still large and was the reason for changing venues, but the dressing rooms were larger. Therefore, I expected people in the venue to be very enclosed.

To prepare, our company's fashion model's and I met at one of our residential properties prior to driving to the venue to drive to the venue together. We arrived in the parking lot at the same time as Sam and his label and they parked behind us, got out of their record label vehicle to walk into the venue, but did not speak to us. For example, Sam did not speak to me, but my vice president pointed out he was standing behind me a few feet away and I slowly turned around to see as I was gathering our luggage out of the trunk of our vehicle. Sam and I had not really spoken in detail since he walked off from conversations at the previous event, but we talked briefly in between other events, so he knew our third year at the show was approaching and the dates of the show.

After Sam and his label existed vehicles they drove in, Sam and his label mates walked a distance behind us, so I know they saw us entering the venue. Upon entering the venue, we were stopped by a few record labels, publishers, and radio stations for interviews and then decided to take a quick restroom break before entering the official venue to be directed to our dressing room and immediately get to work. During this time Sam had time to speak to me and our talent as well as call me on my mobile phone, in general, and regarding the show.

As the fashion models and I headed into the venue where the awards show was scheduled to be held to meet with the chief executive officer of the production company, so he could show us to our dressing rooms, Sam and his label mates came up behind us trying to enter the venue without admission tickets. The problem with this was, usually everyone who attend the awards show each year knew the event cost financially to enter, unless you were given a free ticket by someone who worked at the event or production company.

> "...Sam's arrival makes me laugh".

Based on Sam's behaviors at events prior and not speaking with him before the third-year awards show, I did not reserve any free tickets for him and members of his record label, which I do not think he communicated to them.

Sam's Behavior Before, During, and After the Event

To paint a picture about Sam and his label mates trying to enter the awards show venue without admission tickets, as my team, fashion models, and I were entering the venue to head to our dressing rooms, Sam and his label mates came up the escalators behind us. I was aware of this because I was looking around at each of the guests arriving and chatting with one another to network. As I think about it now, Sam's arrival makes me laugh because Sam and the members of his band and label mates were looking around for what to do next. As I prepared to head to our dressing room, the production company CEO headed towards my staff and I and advised the venue attendant we were okay to let in for free and were event staff. Next, I saw Sam and members of his label approaching the venue and saw the venue attendant slightly approach them with a demeanor of preparing to ask them to present tickets for entrance. As this was happening, my team, fashion models, and I walked into the venue to move forward with work for the day.

    When we got to our dressing rooms I texted message Sam on his cell phone to see if he was okay, was able to enter the event, and that I could not be around to assist him at the show with anything or wait around to see what was going on because members of my firm had work to do, more responsibilities at the present show than previous years. Sam did not respond to the message. His cell phone was probably off, or he was ignoring the messages. I perceived he was ignoring the messages and the perception was confirmed over time when I was visiting colleagues in his city for other events our organization produced or was a part of producing and Sam had no events planned.

    Yet, there was an occasion in Sam and I's friendship where we were talking on the phone one day in a casual conversation friends engage in and I asked him if he was shy and he said yes. His behavior at industry and our company events and when events were not happening was still unprofessional for a business setting. Mainly, I believed Sam had very serious communication problems and wondered if the issues stemmed from his childhood, past associations or business partnerships that did not go well, or romantic relationships that ended gravely. Poor communication skills can initiate trust, rapport building, and credibility dilemmas.

Nonetheless, the evening was going well, and celebrity and non-celebrity guests were arriving. Prior to the show beginning our staff and talent left our dressing rooms after getting ready for the show and were able to take photograph's with print publications, various individuals, and participate in brief interviews again. During this time, I did see Sam (although I was not looking for him) and his label mates outside of the venue speaking with different attendees, so I knew he was still at the event.

The awards show was getting ready to begin and awards show staff began getting into job roles assigned. Everything was extremely exciting, and I was ready to work for the evening. Then, I received a surprised visit from fashion models I knew from previous year's events I worked with on events and that toured the country, and from celebrity acquaintances from Chicago when our organization first started. I initially did not recognize them, but started a conversation with one of the celebrity guests when he sat down next to me to prepare to perform on stage with his group. His other group members were speaking with our firm's talent and vice president, so I thought the time was right to spark up a conversation.

When he told me his name, I almost fell onto the floor, but gathered myself and began explaining who I was. We were both baffled, and he immediately called his label mates over to explain the situation. Hugs and smiles followed, and other regional celebrity and non-celebrity guests walked around us and watched as we had our little reunion. Additionally, a few of our other twin sets of fashion model talent from another state were present to receive awards for the evening and was one of the highlights of my night to see them in-person because I only get to see them a few times a year since we work in distinct locations. After hugs, chit chat, and smiling for photographs with the them, celebrity guest's performances were starting. Print publication editors and journalists were present to capture the moments and attendees receiving awards, while also taking photographs of our staff and talent.

    Afterwards, I sat down again to take a rest, so my feet would not hurt from wearing stilettos. Most of our entertainment divisions events lasted for three days at minimum to an entire week and our staff and talent were typically on our feet, in heels, for 13 to 17 hours a day. Before receiving his award for his work in the industry, a celebrity guest came to sit down next to me because his name would be called next for an award. A journalist immediately came over to us to capture the photograph and a photograph of my vice president and I for publication. All I could think about was God and I hoped every strand of my hair was in place, which they were.

    I began thinking about God and all He had done for our entertainment arm since music video productions in downtown Minneapolis in 2004, what I had accomplished, and people I had met since entering the entertainment (and fashion) industry in 1993 when my cousin introduced me and revealed talents to me God had placed on my life. So, she became my manager and three dance groups, one signing group, later a pianist, working high-level fashion runway shows, being in front of top agents of major modeling agencies, being signed to nine agencies myself since entering the fashion and entertainment industries, attending mega conferences at the age of 11 with my cousin as my manager, becoming a manager myself and then an agent, and later to meeting my celebrity acquaintances in Chicago, I am still here.

With all of this in mind, I knew my colleagues coming from Chicago to perform at the awards show and that we were in the same room, at the same time, and speaking was not a coincidence. God had already been speaking with me about transitioning from secular work to using the businesses He had given me to work for Him and His purposes, even at a secular event, but with a different agenda. I had already agreed, but was trying to fathom in my mind what God meant and what the transition process involved. Years later, I found out the transition process was excruciating and involved immense spiritual and natural training for character development, self-assessment, more company restructuring, yet capitalizing on the work already completed and adding new capabilities to firm, learning about my purpose in life as a leader of organizations and the nations God wanted me established in, attending a newly launched Christian-based *Destiny School*, receiving Gods counsel and correction about allowing people to remain in my life or around me whom are dead weight, bear no fruit, and ride the coat tails of my career, learning about my leadership style, executive leadership development, changing my network of colleagues from individuals I had known for 5, 15, 20, and even 30 years to new acquaintances, and adversities I never saw coming. However, the pains were worth it to get me to where God needed me to be and is a subject discussed in another book of mine.

For example, my network of connections, with Gods direction and a shift in my mind-set to only thinking destiny thoughts and being connected to individuals aligned with my purpose, assignment, and destiny in life, changed from being balanced between 50% private and public company board directors, company executives, doctors, and community leaders and 50% mid-level managers of firms and a host of subordinates in organizations to 98% board directors, executives of companies, prominent leaders and managers in firms, doctors, and community leaders. Some of the individuals within the 98% range have five to seven academic degrees and many with roles of executive vice president, senior counsel (attorney), vice president, chief executive officer, board member, board of trustees, chief human resources officer, managing director, chair of board, corporate secretary, chief financial officer, senior vice president, president, airline captain, partner, chief risk, revenue, merchandising, people, diversity, digital, investment, marketing, operating, or credit officer, head of asset management, principal, commissioner, investor, executive director, and so on. Some of their professional experience is in mergers and acquisitions, real estate, regulatory affairs, joint ventures, securities, aerospace, human and organizational performance, and change management. They founded, own, work for, or have top executive or top leadership experience at major financial, credit card, investment, stock exchange, clothing retailer, book store, shoe retailer, home loan bank, children's toy store, luxury automobile manufacturing, venture capital, advisory, hotel, hospital, law, computer and information technology, airline and airline technology venture, Olympic, university, actuary, consulting, coffee, restaurant, and advertising and marketing corporations in an assortment of nations, primarily in countries I work in. These executives and corporate leaders do $5M, $8M, $50M, and some a valuation of $2.2B deals along with some of the executives and leaders possessing $2.4B-$23B in profit and loss (P&L) responsibility.

  The host of subordinates I should not have been aligned with were servers at restaurants, sometimes unemployed, in entry-level organizational positions, spent a lot time in hearsay incidents, and were people who stated they were comfortable with living in 700-1200 square foot tiny *houses* (not an apartment, but a house) or $8.00/hour jobs, but complain about personal debts. Too, this section of the book is not meant to be offensive to anyone in any job position but to make a point about purpose and network alignment. Similarly, a job title does not holistically define a person, but in the past, I liked to befriend a lot of people and as I mentioned at the start of the book, help them advance in life and their careers by exposing them to new opportunities, people, places, and things. However, you cannot do this for everyone and need to discern who and who not to do this for and let into your network, circle, life, or even home, which is discussed more throughout the book.

Nevertheless, I did not have an issue with God asking, really telling me and promoting me to work for Him because the purpose He had placed on my life and gifts inside of me where His and I have been prophetic, apostolic, and what we call in church, a *seer* to have divine insight, hindsight, and foresight about people, places, and things since I was two years old. Inclusive, I learned from an acquaintance that you do not tell God no, He owns everything. And to be simplistic, apostolic in the Kingdom of God basically means entrepreneur in the world. Apostles have a purpose of leadership and build or help strengthen existing companies or churches, but mainly build or establish the organization(s), within specific territories, regions, or nations. We are basically serial entrepreneurs. If you consider famous conglomerate businesses or serial entrepreneurs, Oprah Winfrey, Martha Stewart, Hearst Corporations, Unilever, and The Procter and Gamble Company (P&G brands) should come to mind. Supplementary, conglomerate establishments are usually multinational or global in scope, operations, connections, clientele, or customer base.

Further, some of my family members are aware that God had always spoken to me and shown me things about people and places since I was a toddler, including how God would allow me to hear people's conversations and schemes to know what was approaching in the future and who's who, whether negative or positive. Some insight was and still is of political figures, family members, people I do not know personally, and individuals who pretended to be friends with me, like the characters in this book. Yet, God's voice can become diminished through sin, wrong associations, lifestyle, and more. Although you can still hear and discern, your spiritual hearing and discernment is not fine-tuned and errors in life can occur.

In thinking about Chicago, I reflected on how the same individuals who inspired me to expand our organization and launch out into the deep with new organizational capabilities and to move into new territories to work with new people where at an event, at a time in my life and career where I was about to *end* one thing and *began* another. I was also thinking about how tell the production company owners who had become my close colleagues, our staff, talent, fashion models, clients, and the like what I was about to do.

Moreover, the time came for the Chicago celebrity guests to perform on stage and I quickly asked them which songs they were going to perform. One of the group members quickly mentioned hit songs to me I absolutely loved and could remember singing when I did not know them personally; I awed and was excited. Each of them turned to look at our staff, fashion models, and other colleagues of mine I knew from previous industry gatherings, and I and invited us on stage with them to perform, as their backup singers and dancers. I quickly agreed and thought it was hilarious, but gathered myself to be professional for the audience; I was ecstatic, and the evening went fantastic. After the performance we took photographs backstage to capture the moment in time. My vice president then looked at me and stated our careers and entertainment division were getting ready to go to a higher level considering the series of events that were taking place and seemed to be divine although she was did not work for our firm when we worked in Chicago.

The awards show ended well, and I did not think about anyone's bad behavior the rest of the night. After successful on-stage performances, our firm's colleagues from Chicago and other acquaintances invited my vice president and I out to dinner. I was interested in going home to go to bed for the evening because I had other events and commissions schedule for the next day. As a result, I told my vice president to go without me and send my gratitude and love to everyone.

Besides, the colleagues from my past she was meeting with respected and were loyal to me and always behaved with professionalism, so someone from the organization had to meet with them. They were also from another city and state and usually when people come into a city, after finishing errands, meetings, or work they like to spend time with people who live in the city. My feet also hurt tremendously and needed soaking. In the end, I felt like I made a good decision and my vice president could handle the dinner meetings with professionalism and provide me with a written, telephone, or in-person report the next day.

SCRIPTURE REFERENCES

Biblical scriptures always help to put people, places, and things into perspective. Following, are scripture references, red flags, and lessons I learned as I reflected on what took place with people I dealt with in chapter two:

- Be very careful about how you treat people because you could wrong someone who is *The Lord's anointed*, causing you to encounter problems later in life. Some individuals *are* of the Christ and anointed by God to do the work they are doing, but have not been fully developed yet, as I was during this time of scandals and betrayals in my life, although I faced many scandals, betrayals, and out-right mischief people *planned*. I can tell you, not one betrayer escaped Gods judgement. God frequently cites in the Word of God (Bible) to touch not His anointed and do His prophets no harm, as a warning. First Samuel 24:6-7 states, "He said to his men, The Lord forbid that I should do this to my master, the Lord's anointed, when he is the anointed of the Lord... So, David checked his men with these words and did not let them rise against Saul. But Saul rose up and left the cave and went on his way".
- First Corinthians 13:11 states, "When I was a child, I talked like a child, I reasoned like a child; now that I have become a man, I am done with childish ways and have put them aside".
- If a tree or human being has leaves it or we should always bear fruit (results) that represent who or what we are claiming to be. If you do not bear fruit of who or what you claim to be you are a phony, indicative of you display counterfeiting fruit or are not bearing fruit at all and God will deal with you, cursing the phony at its roots. Mark 11:13-14 exemplifies this well and

elucidates, "And seeing in the distance a fig tree [covered] with leaves, He went to see if He could find any [fruit] on it [for in the fig tree the fruit appears at the same time as the leaves]. But when He came up to it, He found nothing but leaves, for the fig season had not yet come... And He said to it, No one ever again shall eat fruit from you. And His disciples were listening [to what He said]". He, in the passage of text is Jesus speaking, to a tree that pretended to have fruit, but when closely examined was not what it appeared to be, tricking anyone not *closely* watching, in general, but most significantly, with spiritual eyes.

- The fig tree scripture reminds me of people who I have seen attend church services, watch a few sermons on television, and deliberately listen to how other people pray so they can mimic the behaviors in front of individuals whom are not mature in Christ to trick and deceive them for the purpose of manipulating them into getting what they want from them, whether financial or materialistic. The gift of discernment is critically important in the world today, critically.
- John 15:16 warrants, "You have not chosen Me, but have chosen you and I have appointed you [I have planted you], that you might go and bear fruit *and* keep on bearing, and that your fruit may be lasting [that it may remain, abide], so that whatever you ask the Father in My Name [as presenting all that I AM], He may give it to you".
- Romans 8:31 conveys, "When then shall we say to [all] this? If God is for us, who [can be] against us? Who can be our foe, if God is on our side"?
- In the Bible, while having dinner Jesus informed Judas, His friend, that at a certain point in time although Judas claimed to be Jesus' friend, Judas was going to

betray Jesus on several occasions. Judas stated he never would do such a thing, but the truth came to pass. For instance, Matthew 26: 23-25 posits, "He replied, He who has [just] dipped his hand in the same dish with Me will betray Me!... The Son of Man is going just as it is written of Him; but woe to that man by whom the Son of Man is betrayed! It would have been better (more profitable and wholesome) for that man if he had never been born!... Judas, the betrayer, said, Surely it is not I, is it, Master? He said to him, You have stated [the fact]".
- Luke 22: 21-22 explicates, "But, behold, the hand of him who is now engaged in betraying Me is with Me on the table... For the Son of Man is going as it has been determined *and* appointed, but woe to that man by whom He is betrayed *and* delivered up"!

RED FLAGS
- Heed warning signs people display in their body language and direct and indirect verbal communication with you.
- I used to hear people say, when people *show* you who they are, believe them. The statement had always been cliché to me, but is true. Throughout the events in chapter two, the behaviors of the individuals validate why the scandal and betrayal pre-meditated against me occurred.

LESSONS LEARNED
- People will not always have your best interest in mind. So, pay attention to discernment, who is the Holy Spirit and is always correct.
- You can give people the benefit of the doubt, but after a while do not continue to put up with people's poor

communication skills or bad behavior, especially adults.
- Poor communication aptitudes and inappropriate actions are signs of other natural and spiritual issues a person has and is likely recognizable by how the person interacts with people other than you.

CHAPTER KEY POINTS

- Never let pettiness or a woman wanting a man or a man seeking to obtain a woman impact your profession, career, work, organizations, income, investments, or flow in life.
- Do not stop flowing, working, or succeeding to accomplish personal or professional goals, dreams, and purposes to attend to, address, or entertain adults who behave like teenagers and do not know how to communicate or have adult verbal face-to-face private conversations about his or her feelings.

PART 2

BETRAYAL AT ITS FINEST

CHAPTER THREE
Me, Me, Me

A prominent pastor associate of mine told me many years ago relationships either add, subtract, divide, or multiply your life. When I researched the definition of reciprocally applying a variety of resources to see if any of the words of *add, subtract, divide,* or *multiply* would be mentioned anywhere, even within a synonym, antonym, or thesaurus definition, none of the words were listed, but I found interesting information. The word reciprocally involves an *agreement* between parties to do similar acts for one another, but the word reciprocator does not involve an agreement[3]. Although the origin of the word reciprocator derives from reciprocal, a reciprocator gives and takes something someone has done for them mutually[4]. And the antonym of reciprocator or reciprocate is owe[5]. Follow me, what I am saying in this chapter, because I am going somewhere with this.

At the least, a reciprocator should add to your life, definitely not subtract or divide. The reciprocator definition could apply to loyalty and the concept of giving and receiving, like on Christmas. Many times, employers have office parties at the workplace during holidays like we had some sort of event for each holiday for each

---

[3] Merriam-Webster, Inc. (2019). *Merriam-Webster dictionary app*. Retrieved from https://play.google.com/store/apps/details?id=com.merriamwebster

[4] Merriam-Webster, Inc. (2019). *Merriam-Webster dictionary app*. Retrieved from https://play.google.com/store/apps/details?id=com.merriamwebster

[5] Merriam-Webster, Inc. (2019). *Merriam-Webster dictionary app [thesaurus]*. Retrieved from https://play.google.com/store/apps/details?id=com.merriamwebster

corporation I worked for in my past. For one major health organization I worked for with medical doctors (M.D.) of a variety of specialties, providers, and insurance carriers after being pre-medicine in college (undergraduate), we had a lot of office events. To change the timing of events and honor employees for work completed and to get to know each other, I assisted with planning some of the office events as an events committee member.

As a member of the committee I represented our administration and the office to give back, pay back, or restitute employees for being loyal to the company to *retain* their employment. Although the company really did not *owe* anything to staff since staff were receiving monetary compensation, fringe benefits, partner rewards, and the like for work performed and no agreement was made between the entity and employees to provide such complimentary events, a knowledge of loyalty and wanting to do something nice for employees who worked hard for the company daily flowed through events committee members. Returning the loyalty was the right thing to do and not mechanical, out of obligation, but was doing something nice just to do it.

When an agreement about a pay back is not established, you never want to make someone feel like they owe you for something, especially in a developing friendship. Yet, how many of us know, after a while, when someone has done a number of great things for you and you see the person putting forth effort to bless you, you *naturally* want to do the same thing in return, bless them, by adding or multiplying to their life, to be positive and show gratitude? The last thing you want to be known for is a loafer, freeloader, or divider. People who usually cause division are negative, plan the division, and conduct division frequently. They repay good with evil.

The thought has crossed my mind several times over the years, does God consider repaying good with evil stealing? An individual who is only interested in receiving instead of giving, especially receiving from the same person, could be a thief. The definition of reciprocator also means to reciprocate continually, not just one time.

Still, to pay back good with good, some of my clients, on the East Coast for example, television networks, television producers, public relation agencies, and a foundation one of my favorite [retired] Philadelphia Eagle of the National Football League started do small things for our corporation to be loyal and show appreciation. At the time of working with these organizations and persons, our entertainment company and model agency (at the time, now an advertising and marketing agency with a talent division) booked work with them. In appreciation, besides monetary compensation, a lot of exposure, and connections, they would send an appreciation email or mail a card in the mail to say *thank you*, include everyone in their offices name and for the holidays send a holiday photo with all of their staff in the picture. Ah! The thought of their kindness warms my heart so much, in general, and to the point where I want to continue working with them. I do the same for people I work with, for family members, for friends, for associates I volunteer with at church, for my spiritual parents, and more. I send them a card for holidays, birthdays, and just because to let them know I appreciate them, and I write on the card *why* I am sending them the card and *why* I appreciate them, to thank them.

> "...retired Philadelphia Eagle"...

Over the course of several events our entertainment division produced, helped produce, were affiliated with, were booked for, or supported, I engaged in reflexive practice to evaluate reciprocators, people who either *added* or *subtracted* from my life and or organizations, which occurred with a black history month event, Sam's record label promotional materials, and a concert Sam produced while he was concerned about losing invested finances. The order of events is deliberated in order of occurrence as much as possible, but may be slightly out of order, yet the principality of each situation is relevant to the context conversed. Inclusive, I did not weigh or clearly recognize *dividers* I was surrounded by at the time, but I believe you will find what I have to say interesting.

A Black History Month Event

A friend of mine who I have known for years, approximately since I was a freshman or sophomore in undergraduate college and explained some business plans to and he expressed mutual interest in, called me on the phone one day to ask me if I would partner with him and two of his colleagues on a Black History Month event he wanted to produce at a Historically Black College & University (HBCU) in his city. He asked if I would travel to his city to set up, attend, and conduct the meetings, and most importantly secure one particular prominent recording artist for the event and ask the artist if his recording studio could be used for one or two of the meetings. I agreed to help produce the event, be the intermediary between my friend and the prominent artist and meetings, book talent, other recording artists, and work with radio stations and clothing retailers for a fashion show segment my friend wanted to create.

Additionally, my friend enlisted my partnership because he knew my work ethic, the black history month event aligned with my work interests at the time, and he was aware of my administrative and organizational skills and industry connections. We agreed I would work on these aspects of the event in addition to the ones abovementioned while he worked on other logistics of the event along with ticketing creation, black history oil painters, t-shirt makers, and shops to sell merchandise at the event. To the event, I also invited entertainment industry colleagues from out of town, clothing designers from our *stores* division of the conglomerate, a notable photographer colleague from another state who had just moved to my friends' state and was starting an urban magazine, Michelle to give her an opportunity, and even Sam and his label since they lived in the city where the production was taking place. In the end, due to transportation issues, Michelle could not attend. Although, our talents were provided for in all booking areas, they were responsible for getting themselves to the black history month event. Later, I recognized I was glad Michelle could not attend, so there would not be any problems.

 Numerous recording artists were considered for the black history month event and we had many meetings to come to a consensus about which labels and artists would perform. Meanwhile, a clothing retailer asked if our agency arm worked with male talent and I said no, but would ensure he had males for his segment of the show. I immediately thought of Sam and his label mates since his company could receive exposure and Sam and I were becoming close friends during the time of the event. So, I telephoned Sam about the opportunity to work with the designer and he said yes, but needed to check with the other leaders of his label and members of his group.

During the event Sam's behavior was extremely questionable. Throughout having everyone practice parts they were assigned for the production, Sam walked back and forth to watch people and things happening in the practice and was attending to his label mates. I supposed trying to get everything squared away with his team. In the middle of practice, I would *text* Sam and he would not respond although I saw him with his phone a few times.

Prior to ending practicing everything, I spoke with one of Sam's label mates in a room of the university venue about me texting Sam and he laughed and essentially steered me in the direction of there were issues with Sam, and this would not be the last time the label mate would indicate this to me. I decided to *walk* over to Sam to speak with him. The brief conversation was about the event, me texting him which he knew nothing about, and advising him he and his team could go eat dinner, food I told Sam on the phone when I spoke with him before the show our company purchased and brought to the event for the fashion models, retailers, Sam and his team, and a few other worker's in attendance to help with numerous logistics of the fashion show production. Every now and then I monitored the room where everyone was eating and eventually noticed Sam and his team where drinking *alcoholic beverages*, which I did not bring. I recall bringing soda, I believe Coca-Cola. Therefore, I took a mental note that Sam always had a red or white cup styrofoam cup in his hand at events.

Nevertheless, Sam did not speak to me much at the event, just watched, and when the event was over he and his label mates hanged around for a little while and then left. On my way out of the university for the evening to meet with my vice president, as I approached my rental vehicle the notable photographer came up behind me calling my name. I turned around to see who it was, did not recognize him, and answered him rudely. Initially, I thought the person was a groupie and wanted to what some people call 'holla at me' regarding obtaining my phone number with the outcome of pursuing a romantic relationship. I thought this because of the city I was in, but was wrong. The photographer told me his name and I immediately changed my behavior and quite frankly, was slightly embarrassed about my unprofessionalism.

He advised he wanted to work with me on other projects and I agreed. Weeks after the event, during a telephone meeting, he brought up my rude actions and I instantly gave him a lengthy apology, explained my behavior, and we discussed business, his work in Texas from when I knew him while I was in graduate school, his plans for starting an urban magazine, and him wanting my help with the publication. Regarding helping him with the print publication, he wanted me to be on staff and help him recruit and hire staff for several positions he created, which I agreed, and later told Sam about just in case he knew of anyone I could hire. My behaviors, apology to him, and frequent *communication* after our incident is what business is supposed to be about. Anything else signals red flags or some type of negative outcome brewing.

Conclusively, the HBCU event was a success by being sold out, individuals were still trying to get into the event during the evening, and everyone a part of the production completed what they were assigned to do. Likewise, there were some issues even though Michelle was not present, but the issues were minimal. One of the local clothing retailers stated one or two of his shirts were missing or stolen and they were shirts that fit males. I asked Sam about the incident and to check with his label mates. Everyone stated they did not know anything about the stolen shirts, I let the dilemma go, spoke with the retailer about the situation, and we remain associates today even though he lost money because of misplaced merchandise.

The Miami retailer a part of our *store's* division stated the same with one of her dresses that fits a female, which later surfaced because the young lady who stole the dress told me it was her and she wanted to return the dress after I asked everyone several times. Correspondingly, the theft did not ruin our Miami retailers' business, we discussed the incident, moved forward because she knew my positive reputation, and I later contacted her about the salon division of her enterprise working with our major national print publication clients in Chicago who produce urban hair magazines and expositions in Atlanta.

I later found out the young lady stole the dress because of her upbringing, lack of sufficiency in life, and not having enough money to purchase clothing and even food. A few weeks later I sent her cash via Wal-Mart or Western Union to purchase groceries that would last her about two weeks and booked her for another local event at a trade center in her city with a prestigious national retailer holding an expo and producing radio commercials, so she could get a paycheck. Yet, she betrayed me.

The aforementioned and Wal-Mart ordeal reminds me of a talent who worked with our New York team with a client we regularly worked with on consumer packaging, advertisements, print publications, and large expositions in New York, New Jersey, Atlanta, and Las Vegas. For one account, the talent needed her paycheck right away for family matters, so I helped her get it in cash and our firm did not take any compensation from her work. On another occasion I transferred her paycheck into cash and wired it to her via Western Union with a representative we frequently worked with because the talent claimed she needed groceries for her husband and son and had ran out. Later, although I thought she was struggling in life, her and her husband, who were starting a church as pastor and co-pastor and trying to secure commercial property for lease (which they secured) took a week-long trip to Jamaica.

God later sat me down and advised me she was one of the persons who I always helped, but was clinging to me, riding my coat tails, and I let her. He stated this was the case with another individual from Minneapolis. The correction, not discipline, from God was true, He told me in love, and I quickly altered my actions with people from then on. Each encounter I had with each person I describe in each chapter of the book taught me something, groomed me, and was necessary for the promotion, advancement, and elevation God was preparing me for next.

All of the individuals let me know they were not supposed to be a part of my next dimension of success, were rocket boosters to where I was going next, and how to handle complexities, strategically, in the future. It was better that I was used, scandalized, betrayed, lied to, and lied on then instead of in my increase. I immensely conversed with and *thank God* on a regular basis for some of the hell, opposition, and adversities people put me through. The hell, opposition, and adversities *trained me* and *developed my character* for the platforms God had next for me, removed disloyal and unfaithful people from my life although it was through affliction, and God was teaching me about who's who and what people do.

Furthermore, after researching Sam after the betrayal I discuss in chapter five, I discovered Sam kept in touch with the notable photographer, met with him for meetings, and the photographer traveled to some of Sam's events to photograph activities and placed the photos on his urban publication website for public viewing. The interesting fact is a betrayal happened, both met through me, and after the betrayal Sam essentially vanished from my life, resurfaced sporadically a few times, which I discuss in chapter seven with an unknown email sender, and never issued an apology or explanation for the betrayal. So, it makes you wonder if the photographer ever asked Sam about me. If he did or did not or if Sam did not discuss me in detail because the conversations were business related only, my name should have still crossed Sam's mind to initiate communication with me about the incident that happened between us and because he met the photographer through my HBCU production.

A Community Event to Raise Awareness

In between the black history month and a community event to be held at a *medical mall* a publicist friend of mine who assisted our entertainment arm with large public relations projects and connections with a great number of newspapers, journals, news broadcasters, and radio stations, called me about to raise HIV/AIDS health awareness in the city Sam lived in. At the time, I was working with clients in various nations. I decided to adjust my schedule to fit her event in because I am passionate about community health events, particularly events focused on obesity, nutrition, fitness, homelessness, shelters, and HIV/AIDS awareness, initiates I was passionate about in undergraduate and worked on as a pre-medicine OB/GYN student, at Howard University, and in Washington DC clinics and partnerships. Shortly before Howard I worked on numerous projects with colleagues via setting up environmental, health, homelessness, immigration, safe house, elderly, HIV/AIDS, women's health, living in a hostel, sexually transmitted diseases education awareness, and youth after school activities initiative's at University of California Berkley, Rust College, and Clark Atlanta. So, I knew the skills such an event required.

The heart of the event my friend wanted to produce was a fashion show to get people in the door to the event and while at the event information about the initiative would be presented to attendees along with informal awareness talks, HIV/AIDS testing via the consideration of using a celebrity basketball players foundation, and handing out additional resources. Production of the event would also give individuals from a variety of industries an opportunity to network, in an interdisciplinary manner.

After pulling together the statistics for HIV/AIDS in the city the event was happening in, so I could better understand the community we would be interacting with, I called Sam, by now, an official friend of mine by this time, to inform him of the event, some of the statistics to back up why I was interested in following through with the event, and that I would be in the city. Sam's reaction to the event was nonchalant, not as supportive as I thought it would be. Maybe he thought I was shunning the city he lived in by reporting the statistics to him, which he did not comment on. Still, Sam stated okay, and he would stop by the event with his brother Tim, but in a roundabout way, seemed to not fully commit to stopping by the event to say hello. Sam's behavior was the same when I arrived in town. Although after some time of meeting with individuals, greeting fashion talent in the city who wanted to meet me, learn about the past agencies I had been signed with, and talk with about what I learned at the agencies, work, and setting up for the community event, I telephoned Sam as a courtesy call to let him know the times of the event, activities, and grand show.

    Overall, after the conversation I did not hear from or see Sam until the next morning when he texted messaged me, not to apologize for not attending, contacting me, or to see if the event was a success, but because his brother Tim knew my vice president from prior years when she moved to their city from Oakland, California and wanted to ask me to ask her if it was okay for him to have her cell phone number to speak with her. I was with my vice president at the time and thought they were both adults so there should not be a problem and either Tim wanted to speak with her about something business related that did not relate to our organization or something personal since he kind of knew her. However, I told Sam I would ask her and get back with him, which I did, via text messaging and then stated I wanted to get some sleep for the day before officially getting up to get dressed, attend a fashion week meeting, advertisement photoshoot, and drive to a city an hour away for a training and another production.

Fashion Week Meeting and Advertisements Photoshoot
    For the fashion week meeting, I was meeting with two of the producers and our main photographer hired to generate advertisements for the production. To prepare for the event we conducted a lot scouting of talent using model calls to meet, evaluate, and see models walk to assess the models previous training. While each of the responsibilities occurred, additional meetings among the

producers, including myself, of the fashion week were held, in Sam's city, as a central meeting point for everyone.

I kept in touch with Sam during this time like I did with everyone I knew in Sam's city because I always let people know when I coming to an area where they live or will be working, to support one another's work, to meet for lunch, coffee, dinner, a conversation, or just to see one another. My colleagues, staff, and clients in Toronto, London, Nigeria, and South Africa, and friends in Kenya feel the same way and say, "Kyla, it is so good to hear your voice". With working under a conglomerate and in many cities our firm is established in, I have to travel for work and do not get to speak with or see everyone I know on a regularly basis, so it feels good to touch base, catch up on conversations, and just be in one another's presence. Therefore, I kept in touch with Sam too because we were friends.

> "...if he was at home...what his address was".

So, after one of our fashion week meetings I texted messaged Sam about going to lunch together and he agreed. I advised him we could either meet or I could pick him up and we could just get a sandwich, chat, and then I needed to leave because I had other work to do in another city, all that day. Sam agreed to me picking him up, but I discerned he was a little uneasy about it, not much, yet agreed to go. When I thought about it, I was not sure if he was at home or not and got the feeling he did not want me to come to his house. I never got the chance to ask him if he was at home or what his address was, so I would know where I was going and to decide on place close to his house for lunch because I began confirming our schedule for the rest of the day with the other fashion week producers and learned they wanted to push one of the advertisement shoots up from a few days later to that day and the next day. The schedule modification was not a problem, so I texted messaged Sam to apologize and let him know I needed to cancel lunch with him because my schedule for the day included more work than I thought. I only had a small amount of time in between completing the schedule, picking up two colleagues and my vice president from a personal meeting she had, and getting to an engagement we had in another city. He was okay with me cancelling, acknowledged sympathy for my schedule, and we agreed to having a phone conversation later.

A Business Training

I was conducting a training in a city near where Sam lived for another company I was launching, but Sam did not know the details of the meeting, the company being launched or business training, and after the training, producing an event. Besides, I did not invite Sam to the event even though the production was not far from where he lived because the show and what my organization was seeking to do next was not related to his line of work. Too, I was right about cancelling lunch with Sam because during the rush to get to our training and the venue for our next event because my vice president forgot her company shirt for work and none of the individuals attending the training and event with us had a lot of time to spare for eating or doing anything else in between.

However, after fashion week meetings, the training, and other work engagements, I remembered I had Sam's new business cards. We spoke at time prior my fashion week meeting and other engagements when I was browsing the Internet and noticed business cards I previously came across that would be great for him and some for myself, where on sale for an extremely low price, nearly 80% off of the original price. He agreed to the ones that would be great for him so when I knew I could order them for a low cost and mine, I immediately told him about the deal and asked him if I should order them. He said yes, so I ordered ours together to catch the sale before it ended.

I called Sam and told him I remembered I had his business cards, could meet him to give them to him, but would need to stay near the interstate because I was tired and heading home for the night. Sam met me in a Hilton Hotel parking lot right off of the interstate. When he arrived, he asked me to get out of the car, we hugged, briefly chatted, and I walked around to the trunk of the rented SUV to retrieve the business cards. He inspected the new business cards and was thrilled that they looked extremely well, were his taste, and thanked me.

After meeting with Sam, I decided to stay in town for the night and drive home the next day. The next day came and Sam text messaged me about working with a prominent record artist who also owns a record label and a large recording studio in Sam's city. Sam asked me if he could drop off some of his promotional materials/music to the label owner within a few hours at least to not wait so long, in hopes of the label owner reviewing his material and possibly working on a project together, whether an event, concert, or album. I was driving somewhere at the time, told Sam I was still in town, and I would ask the label owner's cousin in charge of opening the studio and get back with him shortly because it was Sunday, a day the label owner does not go to the studio, but his cousin goes there at exactly 2:00pm to open the studio for people who meet there at that time and one of the persons was me. Within a few seconds of text messaging the label owner's cousin he texted me back to confirm he was still going to the studio at 2:00pm and Sam could come by. I told Sam the information, he already knew the address to the studio, and I stated I was not going to the studio at 2:00pm because I needed to go home.

At the conclusion of Sam and I's discussion about the studio we started discussing a personal matter. I believe I started the conversation and currently do not remember all of the details, but the conversation revolved around a few people Sam knew and was either hanging out with or trying to do business with and I was bringing the information to Sam's attention. One of the gentlemen was telling me some things about Sam, his behaviors, and would ask me on various occasions why I dealt with Sam. I told Sam about this and asked Sam questions about it, including why the person *he knew* we were talking about would say such a thing. Sam did know and did not want to answer some of the questions, which aggravated me. The conversation ended abruptly when I told Sam he has a listening problem, does not listen to me as his close friend when I am trying to explain something to him or warn him of someone, and I hung up the phone on him to drive home.

I also hung up the phone on Sam because I was tired of guiding conversations with him to get answers to a lot of thing that were confusing about our association, with the main question being what kind of friendship were we in? When I got home, I called Sam to apologize for my actions, briefly explained why I hung up on, and told him it would not happen again and was out of character. Sam genuinely stated he accepted my apology, just did not want to be talked to in a negative manner, and he wanted me to watch my mouth, the words I spoke. We chatted for a moment and I mentioned I wanted to take a nap and we ended the conversation there.

The next time I spoke with Sam was when I was in Nashville to work on set of the television show Gospel Dream. Michelle Williams, J. Moss, and Mary Mary's ex-manager Mitchell Solarek were judge's that week for the Gospel Music Channel broadcast, during a Melinda Watts segment when the casting director asked me to be a front row audience member. I agreed to support the broadcasting and is the reason why I went to Nashville. I later spoke with Sam while in a city near Memphis when working on a major motion picture with an MTV producer from Los Angeles. Sam and I's conversations were only chit chat and there did not seem to be any problems. Yet Sam seemed to be skeptical about the Nashville taping, but had better behavior when I was talking with him on the phone during the major motion picture taping and was probably because he could hear the actors and producers in the background, information vital for understanding how everything mentioned in chapter three comes together at the end of the chapter.

Record Label Promotional Materials

One day Sam called me, and we discussed industry events and what he wanted to work on next for his record label. He was attempting to work with individuals, venues, and event producers *locally*. At the time I was working on two events in his city, one was fashion related and the other was recording artist related. For the fashion event, I was only assisting with the event and brining in fashion models as talent, but for the recording artist event, I invited Sam and had a lineup of performances.

Sam began discussing his career with me and the conversation was not unusual because I asked a few times in the past about his five-year plan, where he saw himself in the future, and we discussed him moving to another city with several cities in mind, places where some of his record label affiliates moved to and where some of his family members or friends live. Some of our conversation revolved around Dallas and Houston, and then New York, Memphis, Nashville, and Atlanta. Each are cities where the entertainment industry, from his perspective, has something going on.

To that extent, Sam asked me if I could check the price of an airline ticket to New York for that week. I did not mind since Sam and I were friends, a New York colleague of mine and I ran an internet radio station streaming music for listeners throughout the day and had celebrity interviews at scheduled times, so I needed to access the Internet after work regularly, and I assumed Sam wanted to travel there for business. Consequently, I told him I would check the airline prices and get back to him. I then waited to see if he was going to ask me any New York business related questions, but he did not, so I moved the conversation along. Also, I recall Sam stating to me at one point in time he needed a new laptop, and this could have been the reasoning for him asking me to check the prices, but I did wonder why he asked *me*?

Nevertheless, I began discussing a Nashville event that was approaching the producers of the award show I frequently invited Sam to were developing around my birthday month because it was one of the producer's birthday month too. The producer wanted to develop an event to celebrate, but more so to create an industry event for networking. Sam was interested in the event and stated his brother Tim's birthday was during the same time, the week before mine. So, I invited them to the event, advised that I had a rough draft of the agenda for individuals from my organization who were attending, and could include his label as special guests on the event, but would need to confirm with the producers. Some of the agenda included a wall signing at one of the awards show producers prominent retail store locations, a paid dinner at a luxury restaurant in a VIP section, radio station developments, a visit to one of the award show producers record store, and other activities.

The purpose of the record store visit was to review how a retail establishment is operated, to connect with the management, and possibly present some of their label's music. At this time, Sam began telling me about how he had syndicated radio air play in Louisiana, airplay of his music in his city, and would like to send me some of his and his labels promotional materials for showing some of my colleagues and possibly radio program directors. I agreed, gave him our firm's postal mailing address to be mailed to my attention, and stated I would need to review the materials first.

After Sam and I's conversation was over, I did not think anything negative about our conversation until a few years later, after the major valentine's day scandal delineated in chapter five. Sam seemed to be highly interested in the business aspect of our friendship, if the business aspect could assist him with his career and advancement of his label's agenda although there seemed to not be a solid plan in place. I began taking mental notes.

Sam's Concert and Losing Invested Finances

Shortly after Sam called me about his promotional material's he texted messaged me while I was on my way out of a meeting to ask me how I was doing, how my day was going, and how was the weather where I lived. I answered his questions, asked him the same, and could tell the chat was genuine. Sam then called me about wanting to have a concert at a venue in Memphis on Beale Street. I do not think the phone call followed the text messages to be cordially and leading, to get me to hold a business conversation. Yet, I did not have long to discuss the event over the phone, so Sam quickly ran the details by me and I agreed to help him promote the event. I also told him I would attend the event with some of my staff, one friend of mine from the East Coast who now lived in the area and is a former pageant sister of mine who would be delighted to attend the event and meet people, and we would support him and his label.

As Sam's friend and since we were becoming close friends, he confided in me about how the event *had to be* successful, primitively sold out because he needed to either make a profit on or break even with the finances he was putting into the concert. Sam definitely did not want to lose finances he was investing into the concert. I assured him, with promotions and support he would be fine, and I would do everything I could to help him. He was relieved and agreed to move forward with planning the concert on his end with his label mates and industry acquaintances who were investing in the event too, some of them I knew.

While Sam was planning the event over the next few weeks, at some point he wanted to know what the venue he chose to hold his concert at looked like and asked if I would drive by to briefly scan the premises and provide feedback to him afterwards. He did state he would be coming into town and would also take a look, but me driving by the event was not a problem since I lived closer to the venue than him. I drove by, scanned the exterior and interior since the doors were open and reported the venue looked well and was appropriate for the type of concert he was producing. Not long after, maybe a month or so Sam's business acquaintances were ready to promote the event, including in person, called me on the phone to let me know, and I assisted.

When reporting the look of the venue to Sam after driving by, I also asked Sam about the theme or attire for the event. There was no set dress code, so I asked him what his favorite color was to make the night of the event special to him. At this point in our friendship, although it may not be completely recognizable by reading a book, based on the reality of how the positive things in our friendship were playing out, I had already developed romantic relationship feelings for Sam, not sexual, just romantic relationship feelings and wanted to date him. A few times I asked Sam if he felt the connection and feelings and Sam stated he had, but did not disclose them fully and stayed away from conversations about explicitly pursing a romantic relationship, but subtly revealed his thought, heart, and feelings like he was treading carefully. Hence, Sam told me the color scheme and I advised him I was going to wear that and chose a dress and Jessica Simpson heels to match.

During the planning of the event I told Sam clearly what I was wearing and the night of the event approximately 15 minutes after I had arrived and stood next to the entrance of the venue waiting to be seated at an open table with my team, Sam walked over to me, with a drink in his hand, hugged me, told me I looked sexy, and then stood back a few feet off to watch me in my new outfit. I laughed, turned around to motion to the doorman and ladies I brought they could come in. We walked over to our table to have a seat, began glancing over the environment, event set up, event attendees, and waited for the show to begin.

Throughout the evening and night, Michelle called me on my mobile phone twice, once to see how the event was going and that she was still working on attending and then later to let me know she could not attend. I advised the ladies sitting at the table with me who was calling, another talent; I always told them who they would be working with or attending an event with. Further, various recording artists performed at the event, including Sam's band. Sam also texted messaged me chit chat throughout the night about where I was, what I was doing, and who I was talking to. The messages were not inappropriate, just friendly, so I decided to ask him how did he know what I was doing at each moment and was he watching from somewhere?

While the conversation was happening one of Sam's acquaintances who was more of a business partner, who invested in and helped plan the event, worked with another business partner who I discerned was interested in me, romantically. I was not interested in him and indicated so in my actions, yet I saw him walk pass me when Sam and I were messaging. The acquaintance then saw me and came back to say hello. I noticed he was wearing the same colors, from head to toe, I was wearing and so was one of his colleagues who was standing behind him. Then I remembered having a conversation with him during the promoting of the event when he asked me what I was wearing for the concert and I told him; he wore something similar, in color, which I believe was to signify something. To remove whatever hinderance the individual was trying to set up between Sam and I, I quickly ended the conversation with him, in

> "...he told me I look sexy, and stood back".

general, and just in case Sam was watching, and continued on with my evening.

Nevertheless, my team and I headed to the ladies room to use the restroom and check our hair, makeup, and clothing, and then went back to our table because some of them wanted to order alcoholic drinks. As soon as we sat down a gentleman came over and complimented me on my appearance and asked if we were getting ready to purchase drinks. I stated yes for the ladies, so he reached into his wallet to pull out money to give to me to pay for the drinks, told us to have a nice evening, and left. A few minutes later he came back and set *a rose* on the table in front of me, smiled, and told me the rose was for me, and left. As you continue reading the book, the series of events, in my opinion, were divinely orchestrated even though I went through affliction. God was still with me.

The ladies ordered the drinks, I selected a drink, and then continued the text messaging conversation with Sam to tell him about the man, money, and *rose*. He asked what drink I ordered, I told him, advised him why I do not drink alcohol due to health concerns, and when the drinks arrived, he instantly appeared to grab my drink before I could put my hands on the glass. I laughed because he knew exactly when the waiter arrived.

Sam's group was up to perform again, and attendees got on the dance floor to dance to the label's songs and interact with the artists on stage. After Sam's group performed again, he texted me to let me know he was going to the roof top terrace where other activities were going on and attendees where having a great time. I followed him there, but lost him due to the crowd in various sections of the venue leading to the rooftop and at the start of the rooftop, and decided to head back to my table for the evening.

Moreover, it was beginning to be extremely late into the evening and my team decided to head home. I advised them I was going to wait on Sam and as they were exiting the venue I saw a table I could sit at to rest my feet and text messaged him about them leaving. Another gentleman then sat down next to me to begin a conversation, a dialogue that turned into a long conversation the man wanted to have, which Sam eventually texted me about because the conversation was long. I found his actions to be interesting.

Upon completion of the successful event, I watched Sam, his business partners, acquaintances, label mates, and crew deconstruct the equipment they brought. When everyone was ready, we got into Sam and his label mates record label trucks and headed to the parking garage where I parked my truck; I brought *my rose* with me. I rode with Sam in the front as he drove, sitting in between him and one of his label mates since there were several us, so everyone could fit. When we got to the parking garage, I put *my rose* on Sam's dashboard to see if he would say anything about it then or later like he was commenting on distinct things I was doing throughout the night. Sam got out with me to help me locate my vehicle while his team drove back out to the street level to the nearest corner near the entrance of the parking garage to wait for us.

Sam and I ended up going up and down the elevator over three levels of the parking garage because I could not remember where I parked. Sam got mad while we were in the elevator and spoke profanity to me as to why he does not deal with me much, somewhat under his breath. I quickly asked him what did he say, and he said he did not say anything and to forget about it? I was offended, but immediately let the offense go and dropped the subject. We found were I parked and got into the vehicle and talked briefly before heading to the garage exit.

When we arrived at the exit, I noticed the payment sign and attendant and told Sam I forgot I had to pay for parking inside of the garage although Sam parked at the back entrance of the actual venue. Sam offered to pay, and I declined because I did not want to look weak, knew he did not want to lose invested finances on the event, and did not want him to be in a financial bind. Yet, I should have let him pay anyway, as a man. At this point, Sam seemed like he could be an *adder*, but being a *subtractor, divider,* or *multiplier* was still questionable.

Upon meeting with Sam's label mates outside of the garage it was raining very hard. Sam asked me if I was going to be okay driving home and if he should follow me to make sure I got there safely. I told him I would be fine. We hugged warmly, smiled at one another, he told me to call or text him when I got home to let him know I was there, I told him the event was a success just like I told him it would be, he stated I was right, smiled again, and then exited my truck and got into his. I did have a difficult time getting home in the rain because I could not see the correct interstate exits and drove on the wrong streets three times, but eventually made it home safely. And Sam never did say anything about *the rose* I left, not that night nor ever.

SCRIPTURE REFERENCES

Biblical scriptures always help to put people, places, and things into perspective. Following, are scripture references, red flags, and lessons I learned as I reflected on what took place with the individual's I dealt with in chapter three at different places and times:

Scandals, Betrayers, & Liars | 87

- Luke 6:38 states, "Give, and [gifts] will be given to you; good measure, pressed down, shaken together, and running over, will they pour into [the pouch formed by] the bosom [of your robe and used as a bag]. For with the measure you deal out [with the measure you use when you confer benefits on others] it will be measured back to you". They in the scripture refers to other people. God is a *multiplier*; not only does the scripture apply to tithes and offering from a church or spiritual standpoint, the scripture applies to how you treat or bless people. To exemplify, if you clean out your closet and provide five suits to women or men who live in a homeless shelter and are being rehabilitated into the workforce, when you need clothing or anything else God will ensure your efforts or compensation is multiplied back to you. Just be sure you have the right motives and you do not give away shoes or clothing to a shelter or hospital to needy children, once, for example, and the rest of time you spend your life betraying, sowing discord, lying on, scandalizing, criticizing, being disloyal to, ignoring, or disrespecting other needy individuals or acquaintances.
- In reviewing Luke 6:38 from a tithes and offering perspective, if God tells you to sow $30 USD into a ministry, child, widow, friend, business, or soup kitchen for a specific reason, a $3000 USD bonus from your employer to make a repair to your home or purchase other things you need could manifest the next week. Or nearly $10,000 in personal or business debts could be paid in full or rescinded if you sow $100. Each case are my own testimonies and not having unforgiveness in my heart qualified me for the blessings. See Isaiah 61:6-7, 9 about eating the wealth

of nations and a double reward, payment, or compensation for the mistreatment.
- How we act directly reveals what is in our hearts. As an exemplification, Luke 6:43-45 conveys "For there is no good (healthy) tree that bears decayed (worthless, stale) fruit, nor on the other hand does a decayed (worthless, sickly) tree bear good fruit... For each tree is known *and* identified by its own fruit; for figs are not gathered from thorn bushes, nor is a cluster of grapes picked from a bramble bush... The upright (honorable, intrinsically good) man out of the good treasure [stored] in his heart produces what is upright (honorable and intrinsically good), and the evil man out of the evil storehouse bring forth that which is depraved (wicked and intrinsically evil); for out of the abundance (overflow) of the heart his mouth speaks". Luke 6:45 is one of my favorite scriptures. If you not only watch what people do, but listen to what they say, you will learn what resides in a person's heart.

RED FLAGS
- If problematic people do not address offense's they caused you, which is equivalent to repentance, deeper issues could be at the root of their behavior and future difficulties in your acquaintance with them is likely to come about.
- Sam would state he was attending something and either would and be late or not stop by at all. When Sam did not stop by, he did not call, answer phone my phone calls or text messages. If he did answer my phone calls, it seemed rare, unless the conversation involved me giving him something or doing something for him. Perhaps Sam wanted to keep our business association and friendship about business, but his

actions and words on many occasions revealed otherwise, provoking *confusion* and mixed signals. Confusion is not of God.
- When a person displays nice behaviors like treating you like a lady, offering to pay for things, hugging you, and then questionable behaviors like using profanity to address you or quickly getting angry about something with you, underneath, there is a problem. A deeper complexity being underneath is identifiable especially if the person previously advised you he or she wants to be treated and talked to in a certain way, wanting you to politely watch your mouth around then.

LESSONS LEARNED

- Within every acquaintance I had with a perpetrator, before they scandalized, betrayed, or lied to or on me, some extensively, they did not address their bad behavior towards me with me. The bad behavior led to future negative actions from each individual, and later, major inappropriate outcomes of anger, rage, profanity, and even outbursts from the perpetrators, signifying behavioral perversions exists within them. To this extent, problems with people need to be immediately addressed by either party. Unless God tells you to remain quiet and not speak on an issues for a particular reason and amount of time, which He had done with me before.
- People will eat your food, smile in your face, attend your events, befriend you for gain, and then bite the hand of the person who fed them. Basically, they will betray you.

CHAPTER KEY POINTS

- Just because you bless someone in some kind of way does not mean they are *interested in* blessing you *or will* bless you. Being interested in a thing and actually doing the thing are two different things.
- A recording artist friend of mine who is young, probably only about 26 now, has a beautiful wife and family, and was a major part in my rededicating my life to Christ when he was approximately 16, told me when he was 21 I have a *good heart*. I met him by God giving me his name while I was working on the logistics for an event in my office one day and came across his music on the radio, asked God how I could contact him, coincidentally sat down next to him while at a church in the city he lives a few weeks later, and we introduced ourselves to one another. Over the years he would repeatedly thank me for things I did for him and his family, which I knew was God because I had many conversations with The Lord about my observation of people always wanting from me, but never thanking me when they receive. With this mind, I realized I do a lot for people who do little for me, inclusive of never thanking me. I have questioned how can someone at his age speak and behave in a mature manner when individuals I know in their 30's, 40's, 50's, and 60's are still operating in scandal, betrayal, lying, greed, and other kinds of wrongdoing in business associations, workplaces, friendships, and wanting things from people, but never giving the same people they want something from something in return? At least a thank you and not just once.

CHAPTER FOUR
Deception and Mind Games

Leaders and followers of leaders possess distinct characteristics. Although industry and organizational level (job title) specific leadership characteristics exist, general characteristics of leaders and leader's followers consist of particular attributes, values, integrity, moral development, skills, expertise, behaviors, strategies of influence, confidence, optimism, and beliefs and assumptions. For example, leaders *actively engage in* developing and mentoring, tactfully resolving conflicts, empowering and encouraging others, practicing integrity and fairness, casting vision, monitoring finances and operations, allocating resources, building teams, strategic thinking, possessing external awareness, and ethics. Further, ethics comes from motives and values.

Moreover, leadership and strategies leaders employ to be effective is situated, still, being ethical and fair should not be situated, but occur at all times. For instance, leaders in Latin America utilize self-awareness and reflection as a leadership strategy to ensure they perform effectively. Latin American leaders routinely look back on their performance in certain areas, to reflect, before moving forward with new agendas, which is what the content of the book helps me with and should help you. Overall, the strategy can assist with enhancing firm competitiveness. I display these characteristics and the ones abovementioned throughout chapter four and within this book.

Comparably, 21st century leadership trends are leaders are more effective when they possess ingenuity and diversity sensitivity where everyone's perspective is taken into consideration. Ingenuity is necessary when organizations are expanding into new markets, are multinational or global in scope, want to remain competitive or develop new products, services, systems or methods to achieve work tasks or solve organizational intricacies, like our conglomerate.

For diversity, diversity helps build mutual trust, respect, relationships, cooperation, and secure resources, which assists with retaining personnel and is necessary for any firm, but I believe is critical for a global entity working with people from an assortment of countries due to company expansion, merges, acquisitions, partnerships, or even joint venture creations. Knowing how to engage in teamwork is significant and needed for 21st century leadership too. A leader who has the capacity to coordinate, collaborate, and strategize is paramount when working with varying divisions, levels, architectures, or subsidiaries of a firm, specifically if work has to occur in different places or states, countries, or time zones, which is what I was and still am engaged in.

At the time of Michelle's orientation meeting for the first awards show I discussed in chapter one, I did not disclose our plans to expand the company. She also did not know we were a conglomerate, but found out many years later, which is where I want to put a pen, if you will. I was basically practicing ingenuity during the first awards show, by signing some of the fashion models on to our entertainment arm as independent contractors while not entering into a written contract with others, like Michelle. The objective of the method was to appraise if the independent contractor method would be practicable.

In considering the approach, I tend to place individuals in a few different categories when assessing them over time through observation, conversations, research, and other strategies. Some people are for you or your organization and will support all endeavors in any way they can. Others will bluntly voice and show disapproval for you, your company, and efforts or ideas.

Meanwhile, there are also people who you have to carefully and strategically take a closer look at over time to learn about their agendas, in general, and what they plan to do by being acquainted with you. I place such individuals in a deception category because they conceal what they want from you, are interested in your career, organization, or success based on what you can do for them, but are not truly for you and will pretend to be to get what they want, using deception, manipulation, mind games, and *staged events*. To paint a picture, I know individuals who have staged their homes to try to fool me, people I know, and person's I am acquainted with into thinking the person is genuine and has one agenda, when in reality they were trying to do something else, and involved serious unethical financial schemes.

Based on personal and professional experience, the time frame to find out what individuals are really about and agendas and motives they possess can happen during three, six, eight, nine, and even twelve months of becoming acquainted with them. Other timeframes are immediately, 60 days, two, three, five, ten, fifteen, and thirty years. The timeframes also vary based on the person's personality. I have learned about people's real agendas from a qualitative standpoint of observing people's personalities and engaging in conversations with them *and* from a quantitative position of reviewing financial statements, monetary capacity, and spending habits.

Other, more simple approaches to finding out if a person is deceitful, manipulative, plays mind games, does or does not favor you or your organization, but exercises pretend behaviors is to monitor the person's behavioral patterns, character, and reputation. Reputation regards what a person says about him or herself and what other people say about him or her. You could listen to information other people stated about the person and what the person says about him or herself, but I prefer to have personal interactions with subjects to learn about them firsthand. Personal interactions allow me to see if how an individual portrays him or herself is true or false compared to who he or she claimed to be, to make an accurate judgement about the individual to know if the person should remain in my life. Sometimes, as I mentioned before, the latter approach can take years, but at least you would have done the work because if you find out later in life you were wrong about the person or company, you could have missed once in a lifetime opportunities or connections, which I discuss in the virgins without oil section of chapter seven. Henceforth, the key to getting to know people is communication, but you also want to include God for discernment, so He can clarify things you uncover.

Michelle's Patterns, Character, and Reputation

When you walk into a room people you know are sitting in and conversations cease, or facial expressions change or look a certain way, you know the conversations were about you. You can also decipher if the discourse was positive or negative by attendee's reactions to your entrance. The same concept applies to speaking with someone on the phone. Although you cannot see the person, you can begin to know how they feel about you or the subject being discussed by what they say, their voice tone, and overall interaction with you. If none of these instances are favorable to correctly knowing how a person feels about you other patterns in their behaviors, character, or reputation will surface. For example, like someone else who was around the individuals at the time of conversations you did not hear pointing out things people in attendance said, to add to a list of things you might be monitoring or should be monitoring about people's patterns of behavior or character, like lying or inappropriate mocking.

In discussing the leadership characteristic of communicating an organizations' values to its members or associates, after arriving at the first awards show, getting settled into our hotel rooms, and engaging in meetings with talent, as a leader I communicated our firm's values and the vision and mission of the entertainment division to everyone, including Michelle. A fashion model that worked with our entertainment arm for years until she had to move to another state and seriously began taking care of her daughter and obligations she forfeited while trying to pursue some of her dreams advised me of Michelle's frequent reiteration of the company's values. I am not sure if Michelle's conversations with her were in a positive or negative manner, but the point is Michelle new our organization was serious about the individuals we worked with and protecting our enterprise's reputation. For example, for fashion models who worked with or were under a written agreement with our entertainment or agency division, associating our institutions name or likeness with nudity or unethical actions was strictly prohibited. The talent who worked with our association and had to move to another stated told me several times months after the initial meetings Michelle would chant, *we wear clothes, we wear clothes* to signify the values or the company, implying Michelle was mocking me. Although a potential red flag, the information came via hearsay.

Over the course of time and a number of events, I began noticing patterns in Michelle's actions and character that aligned with what the other talent stated Michelle said, causing a negative reputation about Michelle to be formed, including based on what I personally experienced with Michelle up to the current point. For example, the main patterns in Michelle's behaviors and character were her initiating or participating in inappropriate actions behind the scenes and later stating she was not involved and did not do what she was being accused of, starting, or engaging in, like spreading gossip lowly. Yet, she would never speak directly to a person she had a concern with. She would also converse with other individuals about a possible problem, but would not initially say anything when other people directly brought up the issue. Further, she was the cause of drama in our entertainment division whether she attended an event or not. Equally, Michelle was absent from more company functions than present, which means complexities were likely initiated by telephone after exchanging contact information with other event attendees or talent.

> "...desire to protection the reputation"...

Our Company's Reputation

As briefly mentioned in chapters two and three, Michelle was not able to attend many of our entertainment division events, at least 98-99% of the events because of her personal life, child she had with her ex-husband and not being able to find a regular babysitter, studies at a university, transportation issues, and job at a restaurant. The main issues regarded transportation and a babysitter, including needing a babysitter while she went to work sometimes, which I discuss more in the Michelle and confrontation section below regarding how I felt sorry for Michelle.

Yet, during this time Michelle was completing fashion photoshoots and posting the photos online, with her ex-husband, twin sister, and top-less with one of her ex-husband's hands covering one of her nipples and one of her hands covering her other nipple. Her breasts were exposed and could be seen, except her nipples. Also, her ex-husband was top-less as well and the photographs with her ex-husband were posted to the Internet ten to 11 months prior to her planning the valentine's day betrayal against me and one to three months before she attended our first awards show. Michelle knew our company values, moral standards, and desire to protect the reputation of the organization, but never mentioned the photographs until I brought them up after the major valentine's day scandal and betrayal.

Just because an organization has set moral standards, principles, or even a formal code of ethics does not mean participants or employees of the company will adhere to ethical or rightful behaviors, which could affect a firm's reputation. The reputation of a company could be affected because people you work or associate with represent the organization. As an example, when people remember Enron and WorldCom they remember the enormous unethical activities of the corporation's executives.

A similar reputation scenario could apply to Michelle's patterns of behavior and character displayed and reputation with other individuals. Whenever a person displays themselves in an inappropriate manner, other people will look at the perpetrator, people, and organizations they are affiliated with to see if the same wrongful behaviors are present. The cliché of bad company corrupts good character is true; a person with bad character can corrupt a good company. And in the field of organizational leadership there is a normative ethics theory called prima facie principles that warrants people who work with or for an organization should behave ethically out of obligation to do so, representing the companies services to external constituents as if the services or company was their own. The proposition is powerful! Matthew 25:23 claims when you are faithful over a few things or what belongs to another person, *then* God will make you ruler or promote you to be over much or to have your own.

Michelle's New Love Interest

Whenever I worked outside of the office, in the field for events, I provided our staff and talent with my personal mobile telephone number. Michelle, called me on the phone one day to tell me she met someone. As described in chapter two, Michelle met a new guy, either at the college she was attending or the restaurant she worked as a server for at the time. I was curious to know more and what he looked like since she began to describe him, was very happy, and sounded like she was moving in a new direction with her life. So, she decided to text message me a photograph of the guy, with his shirt off, to confirm she had met someone and that he was extremely handsome.

When I saw the photograph, I agreed that he was extremely handsome and our association began to grow into an odd friendship as we continued the telephone conversation, and additional telephone conversations after that one, sharing personal information. For instance, I would share family struggles I overcame, like with my mother, to witness to Michelle who was presently going through the same issues with her mother and needed guidance. We also discussed men and relationships.

However, the conversations were not *as* odd because our firm worked as a family and encouragement, empowerment, and supporting everyone's growth and success in the industry was a part of our entertainment arm agenda. Yet, the friendship *was* odd and in a number of ways inappropriate based on red flags and discernment I ignored on numerous occasions regarding prior company events Michelle attended.

At some point during Michelle and I's personal and professional conversations, Michelle advised me she wanted to have a good relationship with the gentleman and start the relationship on a Christian foundation, which meant conversations, courting, spending time together, and perhaps dinners, but not having sexual intercourse. During this time Michelle discussed with me how her ex-husband she has a daughter with would still come over to her house to talk and on one occasion she had put him out of her house by telling him to get out, when it was raining. I told her if her ex-husband was not treating or speaking to her properly, she had the right to move on from him.

Still, I was unsure of if her ex-husband only came over to have conversations about their child or if he was interested in dating her again. I should have asked to clarify and get a better understanding of the type of female I was speaking to on the phone. For example, a short time after the previous telephone conversations between Michelle and I, Michelle mentioned she gave in to the new gentleman she was seeing and had sexual intercourse with him and tried to speak to him the next day and a few days after that to recommend they slow the relationship down, but could not get a hold of him. She needed someone to talk to because the gentleman seemed as if all he wanted was to sleep with Michelle and if successful, he would move on. So, since she needed someone to talk to, I decided to be there for her when in actuality it should have been someone else.

I Talked Too Much, Too Soon, & Trusted Too Early
Throughout the time of our conversations, Michelle began telling me about her studies at the university she was attending. She was working towards a bachelor's degree in marketing, doing small presentations about our firm at her school because she admired us, and wanted to work in marketing someday. At the time of our conversation we were developing a marketing department for all of marketing functions to flow through, to shift some of the oversight work responsibilities I had, and later to house our marketing department in New York. I advised Michelle I was working on developing a Marketing Director position and I could consider her. Her presentations at her university added to the consideration since she would already have material to present to me to convey what she was learning.

In addition, Michelle confided in me about how she could not attend a large portion of our company's entertainment arm events because she needed a reliable car, a new car. I advised Michelle she could save some money and seek to purchase a new or used vehicle, and use the money saved as a small down payment and to save money she could work more on the weekend's since she was likely going to school during the week. Michelle then mentioned her daughter and not having anyone to take care of her while she was at work. I suggested if she really needed help, I could help her out a few times and she could drive to my home and leave her daughter with me on the weekends, Friday until Sunday night since I lived two hours from her, while she worked and to save money quickly. Michelle stated she would consider the gesture, but was still trying to work some things out.

    At the time I was only thinking about assisting Michelle, so she could quickly get back on her feet in life, but when I consider things I offered her, like with helping her with her daughter on the weekends, my recommendations were foolish, from an executive employee relationship standpoint and from a legal standpoint. I was also too friendly with her and discussed too much personal information, about my life and hers, getting caught up in her problems and mixing professional and personal information and should not have.

    To demonstrate, at one point I also discussed Sam and his interest in me. Michelle suggested we should all take a vacation, all meaning her new love interest at the time, and Sam and me. I advised Michelle that Sam and I could not because we had financial discussions regularly, from personal, not business standpoints, and agreed we would focus on saving finances and doing well financially to be successful in life. Sam also mentioned his credit cards and some of his debts to me, but I did not tell Michelle any of this information.

    The point is I told Michelle too much information, too soon, and trusted her too early with personal information considering the valentine's day scandal and Nassau Bahamas trip that happened not long after, discussed in chapters five and six. Also, I did not think about it at the time, but how could a vacation happen when her new love interest was already becoming a problem, she did not have reliable transportation, probably a small amount of money, no concrete babysitter, and rarely attended company events, aspects about *a vacation* I should have immediately picked up on instead of being buried in my work, too nice, and concerned with helping others?

Michelle and Confrontation

As I state before, implicitly, I should have gotten to know Michelle better by learning more about here before engaging in certain personal conversations with her. For example, the route Michelle engaged in to betray me was similar, but not exactly the same, to how she treated other women, women who were supposed to be her friends. For example, one day Michelle called me on the phone to complain about people not liking her, having trouble with some of her female friends. I wanted to hear her out and offer any advice I could as a leader in an organization she worked with.

Michelle told me how she met with some of her friends for dinner at the restaurant she worked for, only the meeting was not an actual meeting of friends getting together like she thought they had planned. The meeting was arranged to confront Michelle about being interested in one of her friend's boyfriends and acting on the interest by pursuing him. Michelle told me she denied the accusations and I advised her she seems like she would never do such a thing, is a good friend, and she focus on the friendships she currently has with genuine people.

Shortly after Michelle's friends confronted her at the restaurant, the exact same incident happened with Michelle's twin sister and husband. Michelle advised me that her sister eventually moved to the far Western part of the state of Tennessee with her husband, but confronted her about allegations her husband made against Michelle. Michelle's twin sister stated her husband told her Michelle came on to him on a few occasions, once in particular at a one of their relative's home. As Michelle was telling me about the altercation and allegations, red flags where all over my chest, my heart, and I knew immediately something was not right about her if her own twin sister and sister's husband was accusing her of similar betrayal behaviors, but I did not convey my thoughts to Michelle and quite honestly, slightly ignored the warning signs. However, I did house the red flags about Michelle's negative personal situations in my spirit and as I stated earlier, began documenting Michelle's inappropriate behaviors concerning work related matters and events. Whenever you are buried in work, a conglomerate of organizations, dealing with personnel, and your own personal and professional matters, you overlook and forget things about people because you are too focused on something else.

    Moreover, this might sound far-fetched to some individuals, but either Michelle was telling the truth about the incidents that occurred or she was making them up just to see what I would say because she was planning a betrayal against me. The latter does not sound far-fetched to me because I have seen people relay what they are going to do to someone, in advance, even to the person they are going to do it to, to get their reaction, which proposes an individual has a psychosocial complexity. To further illustrate, one day after work while it was still early in the evening I was driving home and decided to stop for dinner. Before ordering my food, Michelle called me on the phone to chat, as friends. I did not mind the casual conversation (and should have) since I was getting ready to order, pay, and collect my food, which Michelle stayed on the phone with me during the entire time, but was not long.

    During our conversation Michelle began talking about Sam, which I did not like and found odd. She started talking about how he seemed interesting and was handsome. My response to her gestures were... okay... and... so what are you saying? She then told me how her and Sam were becoming good friends, had kept in touch since the first or second awards show, he calls her on the phone, and was interested in her.

    To address some of the things she was saying I told her Sam's interest in her was impossible since I spoke with him all of the time now, we were close friends, he told me he was interested in me, and more privately, had begun calling me his baby, "b" for short, while in public at work events, but to mask what he was saying to be professional in front of other people. Michelle then stated he calls her "b" as well and started slightly laughing. Her conversation seemed as if she was hinting at something, but was really unfitting. Personal and professional connection with Michelle should have been severed at the time, but I decided to keep her around to see what would happen next, ended the conversation politely, and hung up the phone in a professional manner. With this in mind, I encourage you to finishing reading the book, in entirety.

Nashville Event and Physical Touching

    I previously discussed the Nashville event with Sam and had his record label name included on the event flier to indicate his label and label mates were attending as special guests. As our entity's special guests, I called Sam on the phone and advised him hotel rooms for members of his label were reserved and paid for. Sam asked me what the name of the hotel was, thanked me, and confirmed his label would be there. I provided him with the information.

    A few days later Sam called me back and stated he called the hotel to check on the rooms for his label and all of the rooms were not listed on the reservation. The tone of voice Sam used was a tone where he was checking on everything to see if I was telling the truth when he could have just stated in our previous phone conversation that he was going to call the hotel to check the reservation. At that time, that particular hotel did not send out email confirmations. I advised Sam everything was under control and I would check into what he was saying, which I did, fixed any issues, and called Sam back to let him know the miscommunication was corrected and his hotel rooms were secured.

On the day of the event some of our colleagues were scheduled to be at a local radio station to do interviews to promote the Nashville event and discuss the organizations. I wanted to get into town on time to stay on schedule, so I called Sam to ensure he was leaving his city at a certain time and would be passing through the city I lived in at a particular time, so we could drive to Nashville together. We all got onto our respective interstates at the times agreed on, including talent with our entertainment division coming into Nashville from Georgia and Alabama.

However, after a short while Sam called me on my cell phone and alerted me that the record label truck they were driving caught a flat tire and needed repairing. He planned to go to a nearby shop to replace the tire. At this point my team and I were ahead of them driving and I asked him if he wanted me to turn around to drive to meet him or pull over on our interstate to wait for him. He stated no to continue moving ahead and he would get the repair completed and paid for as quickly as possible and call me back to let me know they were okay and back on the road again. I agreed.

During the time the flat tire situation was happening and my team and I were on the road to

Nashville, Michelle called me on my cell phone to inquire about the event and advise me that her half-brother from another state, the one I knew from our first awards show, really wanted to attend and planned to fly into Nashville on a last minute flight. Then, she let me know she was not able to attend. While we were speaking, her brother called me on the other line and wanted to discuss the event, so I hung up with Michelle to answer his call, which came in conveniently as Michelle and I were talking.

Michelle's brother started telling me about his excitement for the event, wanting to network with prominent individuals in the industry at the event, and his plan to fly into Nashville and rent a car for the day. I told him that would be fine because the event is not invitation only, but open to the public. He agreed to book his airline reservation to fly in that night and then asked me about hotel room bookings. I advised him he was at liberty to book his own room. He proceeded to say Michelle told him I booked a room for him.

I instantly got angry because of what happened at the first awards show with him, Michelle, and the hotel rooms and told him our firm only books rooms for our staff and possibly any special guests of ours I invite. He got angry back at me and began telling me he did not mind our firm booking rooms only for our staff, but was inquiring because Michelle told him his reservation was made. I advised him he needed to speak with her because the statement was untrue and told him I would speak with her as well and needed to do so right away. When I called Michelle back, she immediately answered. I told her what was going on with her brother, which she stated, 'uh huh', I did not tell him you had a hotel room booked for him through your company. Humorously, I was speaking with two siblings and both seemed to be lying on each other;

either he was lying on Michelle or Michelle was lying to me about what she told him, but either way I was being lied to.

Michelle was always lying about something, so I did not believe her and stated her brother said she came up with the idea and now she is saying the incident is his fault, two siblings saying each other are at fault. After I said this, she did not say anything. I then remembered our special guests, Sam and members of his label and told Michelle I might speak with her again about the incident later, but needed to go. Quickly, I called Michelle's brother back on the telephone number he called me on, apologized for the miscommunication, explained how our organization works, who we work with, and he was not a contracted recording artist nor affiliated with our administration nor entertainment division in any way and needed to make his own travel and lodging arrangements for the event. We conclude our conversation and I moved on to more important matters by calling on Sam to check on him and his label mates. Sam advised they were just finishing up with the repairs to the truck's tire and were going to be on the road within minutes and would call me back to confirm, which he did.

Prior to the Nashville event, our first day in Nashville included activities for our team and then a visit to a colleagues' retail store to sign a celebrity wall of visitors and have Sam's label music played. Sam was able to sign his label's name to the wall as well. As my team and talent signed the wall, photographs were taken and then we prepared to retire in our hotel rooms before meeting my awards show colleagues for dinner at a luxury sushi restaurant.

During our first day there, Sam's label mates propped one of their hotel room doors open to watch everyone who went by, including me. When I would walk by, each of them, except Sam, would yell whoo hooo like they had just seen a beautiful woman. Sam just laughed each time and so did I, although the first time I was surprised because I did not know what was happening. Nevertheless, the dinner went well, we were seated in VIP, my colleagues ensured Sam and his label had a good time, and my colleagues paid the tab.

For the prime event, our attire was royal blue dresses and the event was great. Prior to leaving Nashville, one of the awards shows producers asked me to stop by one of the stores he owns since we rarely saw one another throughout the year, and I agreed. I advised him I was bringing our special guests as well, so they could see how the store is run and to meet him personally. He stated bringing them was okay.

During the record store visit Sam was able to play some of the music from his label in the store and promote some of his other projects. I also introduced his label members to my colleague. Before leaving the store, my colleague chatted with me about my career, what he saw next for me, and congratulated me on some of the work I was doing in the industry. I always felt inspired when he spoke with me about work.

As we were leaving the store, driving in our own vehicles, I called Sam on his cell phone and told him I wanted to visit a friend who was a co-worker of mine from my corporate America days in Minneapolis when we worked with physicians, and asked if he would mind if we made a quick stop? He stated the stop would not be a problem and agreed to follow us to her home. When we arrived, she came outside to meet me, we hugged, laughed, and walked inside of her home to briefly chat. She gave me a quick tour and advised her husband and son, whom I knew, were not there, but showed me pictures of her son and how he had grown. I only stayed inside for about 15 minutes to be respectful of everyone's time and then we went back outside to talk.

After our conversation she went back inside and at that point everyone was out of their vehicles chatting and laughing, enjoying the moment before getting back on the interstate. I wanted to know what everyone was talking about and proceeding to ask Sam, while he walked over to my vehicle to stand next to me. Instead of Sam standing next to me he leaned against the rental car and pulled me into his arms to put his arms around me. I let him; Sam always gave tight, warm, loving hugs and I got wrapped up in the moment. We hug and snuggled, and smiled at one another.

Shortly after, one of Sam's label mates approached us and slightly moved one of Sam's hands from my waist down to my buttock's as he walked by. Sam gave the impression that he was unsure of what his colleague was doing, but left his hand there. And although the gesture made me slightly uncomfortable, I let it go on. I was slightly uncomfortable because I was not interested in a sexual relationship with Sam and we were not dating. Yet, I was comfortable with Sam because I knew him by then and had been around him enough to know he would not try to do anything beyond that, in an inappropriate physical way, including in public. Still, to bring whatever was happening between us to a close, I stated we needed to get on the road, so we could get back to our respective cities before dark.

After arriving in a city one our talent lived in, Sam and his label mates followed me to her drop off point where her fiancé was waiting for her. We said our good-byes, chatted, and took photographs with Sam and his label. As she was leaving, Sam told me he needed to pay a cell phone bill for one of his cell phones and which carrier the phone was under. I told him one of the carrier's stores was near my house and I could show him where and asked Sam if he wanted to ride in the car with me? He agreed to ride with me and told his team to follow us, in an unusual way. I was not going to kidnap him.

When we arrived at the mobile carrier store, Sam and I sat outside of the store in the car for a few moments and talked. Towards the end of our conversation we discussed the nickname of "b", meaning immaturely Sam was my baby and I was his. Sam then stated, he needed to go into the store to get the bill taken care of. I said, well okay, and by the way, how much is it? He stated around $80.00 and proceeded to laugh and asked me if I was going to take care of my baby's cell phone bill and I said no.

I knew Sam was joking, but he also seemed serious. If I was going to take him up on the offer, he seemed like he would not have refused. Simultaneously, I thought in my mind, a man can pay his own bills, he was just a special guest on my event with VIP treatment at every activity we did, and consider the behaviors he has displayed off and on throughout the course of knowing him. In addition, I was not his wife to be able to pay his bill and even if I was, God purposed men to be providers.

While still smiling he got out of the car to go pay and then into the truck with his label mates who parked beside us. He called me on the phone to let me know they were heading home, and we said our goodbyes. I told him I would text message him to let me know I made it home safely, was in my garage, and then walking into the door of my home, which I did.

Sam's Birthday's, Meetings, Studio Visits, & Being Out of Town

Something I found to be interesting about Sam was I only recall him telling me happy birthday for my birthday once and he probably did so because I was on the phone with him at the time and reminded him about a week before. Dissimilarly, I told Sam happy birthday every year and sent him a card. I have never really shopped for gifts for a male before, only on rare occasions, like for a family member and decided I would send a card or a card with cash so Sam could purchase his own gift, something he liked.

One year I remember asking Sam what he wanted for his birthday and he mentioned a certain pair of shoes and emailed me the link to the shoe store website, so I could see the shoes. When I began searching the website and came across what he wanted me to see I immediately saw the price and asked him if those were the shoes and he stated yes. The shoes cost a little over $400, like $425.00 and I screamed no, even though luxury female shoes cost the same or more. Though, firstly, I would only spend that amount of money on my husband and secondly, we are talking about a birthday gift for a friend, which a card is suitable enough. I asked him what about if I just send you some cologne and he conveyed he already had quite a few, so I just sent him a card and $100.

In considering the conversations, I find three things to be striking, one what I could do with $425.00 business wise with investments and opening several new corporations to flip the $425.00 into more figures, second if a person purchases shoes that cost that amount and more on a regular basis (which Sam did), why did he not send me anything for my birthday's and jokingly asked me to pay his cell phone bill, and three, why was he worried about losing invested finances for his concert at the Beale Street venue? By selling several pairs of expensive shoes he already had that cost $400 and over would be reasonable to do if he was worried about not having finances for business or personal expenses. Sam seemed to be more of a shoe collector than investor. And each time money was accumulated from work and the consideration of obtaining another pair of shoes arose, instead of securing the shoes an investment should have been made. Where and how are different discussions, so I do not give away non-stock and non-securities extensive advice for free?

    I remember a few years after I started my first two businesses and was working on my next one, I realized I needed to shift my mindset, money, and how I thought about business growth and began to sacrifice hair and nail appointments, purchasing the latest fashions and shoes, and traveling just for fun to not only expand the organizations, but to accelerate growth using a different approach. YouTube videos and wigs became my go to for a little while to learn how to do my own hair and nails and I started mixing outfits and shoes to decrease personal spending.

    In conversation with my maternal grandmother one day about finances and how a female relative of mind spent money on shoes too often, my grandmother and I had a laughing moment about my grandmother stating, "you can only wear one pair of shoes at a time, so why buy more than one pair, at a time, on a regular basis, thinking you can wear them all often"? Her commentary was true. After Sam purchased the shoes, besides wearing them for comfort, fashion, or to boast, the shoes did not seem to serve any other monetary or professional growth purposes and as a result, I viewed them as illogicality.

Meanwhile, several incidents happened where I would call Sam to chat, like he did with me, or would call Sam to let him know I was in his city for work and we should get together, and Sam would not answer his phone, still. For some of the incidents he would text me back later in the day and sometimes late at night to let me know he was or is currently in a meeting or at the studio. The timing of the meetings and studio visits were questionable because he seemed like he was avoiding me more than just not answering his phone, because of record label work.

To typify, one time I called Sam and he did not answer, and I discerned he was purposefully not answering. I was with a relative at the time and asked her if I could use her mobile phone to make a quick phone call and called Sam from her phone number, he instantaneously answered. After he answered I told him it was me, how I had previously called, and why I was calling from a relative's phone number. He seemed to have gotten upset and abruptly stated he did not answer because he was in the studio. When I think about the incident now, I find it extremely hilarious… and childish.

Inclusive, on another occasion a prominent promoter in the Midwest invited me to one of his events and I invited Sam and his label to attend and meet the promoter. Here I am again, trying to help Sam advance his career and company. Miraculously I ended up driving behind Sam's record label truck on the highway getting ready to get off on the exit to the venue. I texted Sam and told him I was driving behind him and provided a description of the scene. At first, he did not respond, until 30-45 minutes later when I was meeting colleagues in the venue parking lot.

Sam called me and told me he and his team continued driving on after the exit to his friend's house in a city named Cordova, Tennessee and they would be coming to the venue soon. They never attended the event. My dealings with him and his organization was either they showed up late or did not show up at all. Too, Sam had a problem with business *and* personal communication.

And to explain my actions, back then, I always gave people the benefit of the doubt. Sam could have been telling the truth or not telling the truth as to why he did not answer calls from my phone number. For example, perhaps he did not answer because we would have carried on a conversation like we usually did, and/or he thought the call from a number he did not recognized could have been a call about a booking for his label mates and promptly answered.

Either way, as I stated, the not answering happened on a variety of occasions and was questionable because of the timing and how Sam behaved. For instance, sometimes when I was in Sam's city and I would call him to let him know and he would be conveniently heading out of town to a neighboring state and did not have time to get together. I mentioned the convenience to him at one point and he seemed to have gotten upset about it and stated he *was* going out of town and mentioned some of the individuals from his label traveling with him. I am not sure if he was truly traveling out of town or not. No information about an upcoming show was displayed on any of his label mates social media like they normally posted, indicating a recent booking, it was unlikely they were all traveling together to see *one* of their family members, and the next thought that crossed my mind was either individuals from the label were going to see a woman, women, or someone was selling drugs. Collectively, Sam's behaviors indicated he did not value or friendship.

I also believe, based on a series of events, Sam formulated his own opinion about me according to what other people (liars) could have been telling him and/or from individuals he was acquainted with perceptions about me, whom knew of me, but did not know me. I discuss this more in chapter seven in the section of virgin's without oil. Overall, after extensive reflection, not only was Michelle deceiving, Sam practiced deception as well, performed mind games, and was not comprehensively straight forward with at all times.

SCRIPTURE REFERENCES

Biblical scriptures always help to put people, places, and things into perspective. Following, are scripture references, red flags, and lessons I learned as I now reflect on what took place with people I kept trying to help in chapter four:

- Regarding liars, Psalm 34:13 states "Keep your tongue from evil and your lips from speaking deceit".
- Throughout the chapter I highlighted how I took mental notes of people's inappropriate actions and against me, gathering information on their behaviors. Isaiah 53:7 mentions something similar during the time of Jesus' crucifixion by His own people (church folk) and so-called friends, "He was oppressed, [yet when] He was afflicted, He was submissive *and* opened not His mouth; like a lamb that is led to the slaughter, and as a sheep before her shearers is dumb, so He opened not His mouth".
- Romans 12:19 says "Beloved, never avenge yourselves, but leave the way open for [God's] wrath; for it is written, Vengeance is Mine, I will repay (requite), says the Lord".

- Romans 12:21 warrants "Do not let yourself be overcome by evil, but overcome (master) evil with good".
- Romans 13:13 states "Let us live *and* conduct ourselves honorably *and* becomingly as in the [open light of] day, not in reveling (carousing) and drunkenness, not in immorality and debauchery (sensuality and licentiousness), not in quarreling and jealousy".
- As I wrote chapter four I recalled 1 Corinthians 12: 8-10 regarding the gifts of the Holy Spirit and prophetic insight in to knowing the events happening to me would be used for my good and to learn about who was authentic, who pretended to be, and how he or she carried out the affectation. The scripture states the gifts are… "To one is given in and through the [Holy] Spirit [the power to speak] a message of wisdom, and to another [the power to express] a word of knowledge *and* understanding according to the same [Holy] Spirit… to another [wonder-working] faith by the same [Holy] Spirit, to another the extraordinary powers of healing by the one Spirit; to another the working of miracles, to another prophetic insight (the gift of interpreting the divine will and purpose); to another the ability to discern *and* distinguish between [the utterances of true] spirits [and false ones], to another various kinds of [unknown] tongues, to another the ability to interpret [such] tongues".

RED FLAGS

- Through various conversations, people, and confrontations Michelle described to me exactly who she was herself. I should have believed her the first time and not ignored the warning signs (red flags).

Scandals, Betrayers, & Liars | 117

- Michelle deliberately *undermined* and secretly *mocked* our company's values to other talent.
- When you believe a lie, you are deceived.
- Sam attempted to treat me the way he wanted to treat me and take my phone calls when they were convenient for him. And although this was information was not listed in the chapter and I advise you to rapidly deal with people who do this to you, at some point Sam advised me he was no longer going to bite his tongue around me. The question is what does this mean and why would you want to bite your tongue around me anyway? Be who you are. If you are inappropriate, *show me*, so you can be removed. Or did you not want to show me because you were more interested in obtaining things from me to help your own label and career as self-interest instead of pursuing external stakeholder interest and reciprocity?
- If you are concerned about starting an organization, increasing the bottom-line of the company you work for, or are interested in partnering with other individuals on distinct projects, *pay attention* to how people and entities who want to be associated with you or you want to be connected to spend money and manage finances. Nowadays research and social media can be applied to identify such information, still people will tell and show you themselves, directly or instinctively.
- Sam had a desire to purchase the last fashionable shoes for hundreds of dollars and do nothing financial wise after the purchase more than acquiring natural knowledge or Wisdom from God about ventures to pursue for long-term growth, legacy, stability, sustainability, social impact, and/or to cure societal ills purposes, using the vehicle of a business or money as a

tool to do so. His desire was an immediate red flag and revealed in his actions.

LESSONS LEARNED

- Extensively research and interview individuals you hire or will be working with short-term while considering them for long-term assignments.
- Consider not only people's work experience before you hire them, but the psychological state of the person as well. Consult legal counsel regarding any employment laws or grey areas.
- People will engage in extensive pretending and have ulterior motives. Apply discernment and act accordingly, swiftly.
- Never allow people into your personal space or life nor tell them too much information about you, too soon. When you do, you give them access. Access for workplace acquaintances should be restricted and is discussed more in chapter six within the section on *beef up security* in your life.

CHAPTER KEY POINTS

- People are not always who they portray themselves to be and will conceal information about themselves or their past from you. Conducting your own research will help uncover what they purposefully disincline to share.
- Pay *very close* attention to what people in your personal and professional life say and do to learn about their patterns of behavior, character, and reputation. When things are revealed, check with God first to confirm, and if He confirms, believe Him.

- Do not wait situations out to see what the outcome will be long after perpetual red flags. I waited because my personality consists of long-suffering, observing, researching, documenting, and is God driven, even at the point in my life when my divine discernment was still being fine-tuned when all of this was happening. Also, only pursue extensive waiting, observing, and putting up with wrongful people if you know there is a divine purpose in it or you want to find out the absolute truth to a situation or person without passing pre-judgement. If you pass judgement on people too soon, even if they act irrationally, you could miss a blessing in disguise. God uses opposition and adversity to grow and promote people.

CHAPTER FIVE
Scandals and Perpetual Betrayals

Do you know the word manipulate is connected to synonyms of abuse, exploit, play, cash in on, pimp, walk on, capitalize on, *deceive*, plot, cheat, defraud, milk, con, *trick*, scheme, and leverage[6]? Each of the words mainly mean someone uses someone else to accomplish a certain purpose. Scandal involves a shocking or blind-sided illegal action or a moral injustice a person or a group of people commit against another person or persons and is associated with offense, reproach, damage, violation, outrage, loss, slander, and discredit.

Comparably, scandal is evil, unjust harm, foul (stinking), defaming, disgustful, wrong, cruel, malicious, and catty[78]. Some of you probably feel like these words describe what happened to you when you encountered a scandal, betrayal, or were lied on or lied to. For example, and based on personal experience, slander and discredit are likely linked to scandal because people who perform scandals typically slander, discredit or *lie about* the individual the scandal is planned against. What I find to be interesting is sin stinks to God and when a person who has not repented for sinning offers up prayers to God or petitions Him about a *need*, blessing, or promise in the Word of God, the prayer stinks to God (see Isaiah 65:5).

---

[6] Merriam-Webster, Inc. (2019). *Merriam-Webster dictionary app*. Retrieved from https://play.google.com/store/apps/details?id=com.merriamwebster

[7] Merriam-Webster, Inc. (2019). *Merriam-Webster dictionary app [thesaurus]*. Retrieved from https://play.google.com/store/apps/details?id=com.merriamwebster

[8] Merriam-Webster, Inc. (2019). *Merriam-Webster dictionary app*. Retrieved from https://play.google.com/store/apps/details?id=com.merriamwebster

As I stated prior, I am originally from a small town in Mississippi, and as a child my cousins and I, and our mothers would pile into family vehicles and drive home every holiday and summer to visit relatives and stay for days, weeks, and then sometimes months for my cousins and me. On the way home, we had to go through many states, cities, and other small towns. In some of those places the air was horrendous and a down-right unbelievably strong bad odor, enough to make a person sick. Most of the bad odors came from farms. I come from generations of farmers, gardeners, and fisherman, until family members in my bloodline began hating the *labor* involved in farming and went into teaching and professorship at local colleges and universities. To this day I am not sure of how some of them survived some of the *smells* that occur on farms.

    I never lived on one of the farm lands, but hated the smell of others and cannot imagine how sin smells to God. Yet, I really wanted to go home for months to be with my friends, attend summer programs, and go to high school dances, even when I was not in high school yet, so I, we tolerated the smells. However, this is different with God and a bad smell is not about fun and games, but about God not wanting to be around foulness. How can a person's prayers be answered when the foul smell causes God to not want to even hear? God not hearing someone is an unfavorable, unprotected, and dangerous position to be in.

    Moreover, over the years I found out people who generate scandalous events will also *lie to* individuals who knew little or nothing about the scandal concerning supplementary events surrounding the scandal, to protect his or her reputation while defaming the person scandalized; scandal can bring discredit upon the person being scandalized. However, after God's vengeance and truth were revealed, major discredit was brought upon the persons who conceptualized the scandal. Consider seminal executives of major corporations in historical and contemporary news media who swindled insurance companies, retirees, small business owners, pension funds, other stakeholders and stockholders, and the like out of millions of dollars to live lavish lifestyles, later to be caught and sent to prison. Natural prisons exist, but God has prisons too, spiritual prisons of bondage, curses, iniquities, no growth or increase, and more to reward people for behaving badly, bringing a disgrace upon others, offending someone, or even making a persons' morals or values who they planned a scandal against, look inappropriate or defamed.

People who plan scandals, betray others, or produce lies can also bring a discredit upon a religion, like Christianity, or God if he or she claims to be a Christian, of the Christ, or of God. Such inappropriate individuals can appear as mockers of a religion or God and should be careful. Pretending to be of a certain religion or God can lead followers or future followers of Christ astray, which God takes *very seriously*.

People who are betrayers tell things unintentionally, leave a person when they are in need, seduce, violate others confidence, use treachery to hand a person over to someone they consider their enemy, tell secrets, are disloyal to and fail friends, *support an enemy, two-time*, double-cross, *sell out*, commit immoral actions, back stab, and hurt someone they know trusts them. Some of you will understand this better, essentially betrayal involves someone *doing you dirty*; a person who betrays is dirty. You have heard about *dirty cops* or leaders on factitious television shows.

Henceforward, perpetual means continuous or to occur often. Perpetrators engage in wrongful or illegal behaviors too, and interestingly, the word perpetrate is synonymous to the words achieve, carry out, and negotiate. Perpetrators usually work with or enlist other perpetrators to help them achieve an immoral action. A major scandal using various circumstances and social media, and perpetual betrayals were performed against me by Michelle, Sam, Tim, and Michelle's cousin.

Lastly, after careful reflective praxis, the perpetual betrayals began and continued after Sam asked me for $200, even though we established a best friend and loyalty agreement. The continuation of betrayals can be recognized by Sam's behaviors over the course of several events, like the creation of nicknames, revealing he has always been interested in me and then stating he had a girlfriend, pretending like he was coming to see me for valentine's day after I attended a friend's wedding, and allowing Michelle to begin do marketing for his record label. Equally, I was going through other betrayals too, concurrently.

Do You Have $200: A Luxury Vehicle

A while after the MTV production, Sam spoke with me over the phone and through text messaging about wanting to work on different events. He also asked about the city I resided in at the time and the type of venues available for urban events. I advised him I lived in an area that was suburban and next to areas considered rural, so conducting any type of event I knew he was interested in was not possible. Nevertheless, I discerned our conversations were not just about investing in or producing an event, but about where I lived, what I was doing, and wanting to come see me. So, Sam asked about this and I told him it was okay to come over. He also conveyed to me he wanted to ask me for $200 he needed right away, and I agreed to give it to him, thinking he was in a small financial bind, but would be okay.

He mentioned he was interested in seeing his friend who lived in a suburb of Memphis at the time he planned to come see me. He told me the day he was coming, and on that day, I decided to complete work and meetings from my home office for the day. Sam arrived in my city early in the day and later that evening said he called me on my cell phone to tell me, but I did not answer so he went to his friends. I told him I likely did not answer because I was in my home office and my mobile phone was not. He was still in the vicinity of where I lived and still wanted to visit me after visiting his friend. I gave him the directions and advised him I lived near the mobile phone carrier store he and I went to after our Nashville event, and his physical touching.

Sam called me on the phone when he was close to my home to reconfirm the directions because he passed the street I lived on by one block. I told him if he passed a certain landmark he went too far. He turned the car around and was sitting at a stop signing in front of my house within a few minutes, I was watching out of the window. As I watched him drive up to the street I lived on and into my drive way I realized he was not in any of his vehicles, a family vehicle he drove to meet me at the Hilton Hotel after my business training I discussed in chapter three, nor any of his record label SUVs, but a silver luxury looking coupe vehicle.

When Sam entered my home, I discovered he brought one of his band disc jockeys with him, one I was not really fond of, which I later told Sam I was not okay with. After they came in, and as usual, when I saw Sam, he gave me a warm, very tight, and semi-long hug. Sam then leaned in to kiss me, smiled, and then pulled away, like he was testing me. I slightly laughed, and we moved on to having a conversation in the living room and discussing records I was listening to at the time, a song by Mary Mary and David Banner and numerous songs I was listening to by DJ Quick. We also briefly discussed a very old event one of my colleagues in Los Angeles had I helped minimally promote, regarding DJ Quick.

During this time, I also pondered how on several occasions I spoke with Sam privately and asked him about what was going on between us, I felt a connection with him, and asked him if he felt a connection with me. Regarding the connection with me, his answer would always be a low yes, but he did not want to go into detail. He stated I have always been interested in you, likely since meeting him on social media after our firm's Kentucky Derby events I discussed in chapter one. I did not address any of the thoughts with Sam and decided to enjoy the night, the conversation.

Late into the evening, unexpectedly, a business colleague of mine, who is now a former colleague, texted messaged me about receiving information about a project she was working on and knew I would have the answer. I began speaking with her and at the same time, Sam and I decided to wrap up the evening. Prior to, Sam wanted an alcoholic beverage, had brought some with him, and asked me if I had anything to *cut* it with or anything to drink. I advised him if he was thirsty, he could get some juice, like cranberry juice or fruit punch from the refrigerator on his own while I carried on my phone conversation. He decided not to because he was actually looking for orange juice or Coca-Cola to *mix* with his drink. I honestly had no idea of what he was referring to because I did not and do not drink alcoholic beverages; Sam and I always had language barriers too.

For example, after Sam and his DJ left, Sam called me on the phone to ask me for the *bread* because he forgot to ask me while at my house. I asked him why he did not eat before he left or if he was hungry I would have made him a sandwich because his drive home was a few hours and so he would not have to make a stop in the middle of the night/morning to get something to eat. Sam advised bread meant money and he was referring to the $200. I told him oh, and I forgot about the $200 because I was busy during the day and it slipped my mind. He stated I could send the $200 electronically using Wal-Mart's money processing services.

I am not sure if Sam saw one of the Wal-Mart stores I lived by when we went to the mobile carrier store after our Nashville event or just assumed nearly every city has a Wal-Mart, but I told him I would electronically send it to him right away in the morning, which I later found out the limit for sending monetary funds to someone via Wal-Mart at that time *was* $200. Immediately, I remembered a football coach friend of mine who just had a new-born baby, lived near my home town, and asked me if I could send him $200 via Wal-Mart. I did not and told him to reconcile his finances with the mother of his child. A similar incident occurred with a family member of mine and someone wanting to *borrow* $200 from her and have the money sent via Wal-Mart. Therefore, all of the individuals knew Wal-Mart had a limit of $200 and I was just finding out.

Nonetheless, I discussed the $200 over the phone with Sam the night he left my house and via text messaging until probably 7am, minimally arguing, but being cordial. The majority of the conversation was about what kind of friendship or relationship we were in.

Not long after, I decided to visit my maternal grandmother in my home town of about 1,500 people to grill burgers on the grill, talk, and sit on the front porch to watch citizens of the town drive by her home like we did every now and then, somewhat close to Sam's city, but not nearly. I told Sam just in case he was having an event, but really to advise him if he needed to contact me he would not have access to me for a while because we do not have cell phone towers in the town, use neighboring towers for reception and Internet, the Internet was only available from the town's small library where we only had two or three computers, and my cell phone never worked there. He said okay, and we went on about our day.

Upon getting ready to leave my grandmother's after spending time with her (and my grandfather), I unexpectedly decided to call Sam on his cell phone from my grandparent's house phone and he quickly answered. He told me he did not try to call me, but if I tried to call him he did not answer over a few days because he was arrested and had been in jail. We briefly discussed how he was doing and to take his mind off of what happened to him I told him I was changing the subject to a non-important matter, talked about ordinary events, and cracked jokes so he could laugh. He told me our conversation was the best conversation he had in a while and was grateful for the talk time because it was casual, making him feel better. Towards the end of our dialogue I asked Sam if he wanted one of my cousins, an attorney with a brother who is an attorney too, both he went to high school with, to help him with his legal matters? I advised him the one who would be willing to help has an office in the heart of his city and is the a few years older than him, while the other lives in New Orleans.

Sam's jail incident reminded me of one of my friends who lives near the very bottom of Mississippi I wrote and sent photographs to for a year when he went to prison, while I lived near Minneapolis. I knew him for nearly 20 years, booked his label for major events, invited them to awards shows, was there for him through two hurricanes in his city and him being stranded on a roof top of one of his friends residential properties, and he later betrayed me by not being present when I was going through something in life and tried to sit him down to talk about it on three or four occasions. He always brushed me off, but knew I wanted to talk to him, so I cut off our friendship without him knowing.

Many years later God *strongly prompted* me several times that my former friend was looking for me and he was. He tried to reconcile after he went through a third hurricane; he conveniently remembered me. I believe he sought reconciliation with me because of my professional life success and because he likely wanted my help financially or for housing assistance, a conclusion I came to, based on research and paperwork I identified about him trying to obtain a housing grant to repair the home he was currently living in with his father, possibly while taking care of his father. I ignored his phone calls to my offices, just like he ignored me and had his calls re-routed. He eventually stopped calling after a year of calling off and on. I find it interesting that after a person has done you dirty how they will go through great lengths to try to contact you, like they need you badly, but totally ignored you when you needed them most.

In another incident, someone who was an associate of mine, not a friend yet, and lived near Sam is a deacon at

Scandals, Betrayers, & Liars | 129

his church and recording artist with a wife and five children. I discerned he wanted to ask me for monetary support for an album he was working on. Instead of asking me right away and directly he launched a campaign through his independent record label and released some of the campaign information in his city, on social media and through email newsletters. Shortly after, he directly approached me about the money. I did not give him an answer right away and ended the association without him knowing, ceasing all contact with him.

Ceasing contact was at an applicable time since I was in the process of changing my telephone number and we were getting ready to work with a new vendor to set up a new telecommunications system for each of our conglomerates offices and nations. Inclusive, whenever he came to a city near where I lived, he sometimes brought his wife, would call me on the phone and tell me they were coming, and then would ignore me for days after they had arrived. I suspected his wife was the issue, she was always rude to me, possibly because insecurity issues exist, but I have no desire to date a married man, a man who belongs to someone else, nor a man who has children, let alone five.

What is funny about the perpetual betrayals I encountered is colleagues of mine in prominent positions in a variety of industries have told me they faced similar, but not the same, financial, friendship, and business betrayals, in many cases betrayals my mouth dropped open about when I heard them. Some of them are prominent pastors with several churches and told me and other colleagues of ours how they would financially provide for people, send those same individuals children birthday gifts, and when those people visited their church they would not speak to *their children, tell them* happy birthday on their birthdays, nor return the gestures. I was shocked about such things happening to them, but after thought, realized the same things happened to me too, from countless people, including on my birthday's.

For instance, while riding in the same vehicle as colleagues *on my birthday*, and at the end of the ride, nonchalantly gave me a gift a colleague who was not in the car bought me. She basically threw me the gift he, my other colleague, bought me. I believe she was very jealous of me in general because the male colleague of mine would brag about how I am the real deal, a real person and never fake, especially in Christ, and people, particularly men are *stupid* for mistreating me. He never said any of that about her. Nonetheless, just because a person does tell you happy birthday does not mean the person likes, supports, or is for you. The birthday wishes were most likely given out of obligation, which God advised me this year after someone gave me a gift for my birthday, someone who I *know* dislikes me very much, equivalent to an extreme hate, but cannot stop the manifestation of my destiny.

Similar events happened to a colleague of mine with several businesses when she invited work associates and guests to her and her husband's main home for an event and dinner. Their main home is a mansion in a gated community and one of the ladies invited spoke to people, but then went to sit outside on the front porch for the remainder of the event. My colleague went outside to retrieve her at one point to tell her not to be shy and she could come inside and enjoy the event with everyone. The lady turned up her nose, turned her head, looked off into the distance, and said okay, maybe. My colleague went back inside, and she said she asked God what was wrong with the lady and what type of manners was she displaying, and God told her the lady cannot stand to see her blessed. I laughed when I consider the situation today, but the lady's manners were terrible, and I feel sorry for her. Jealousy can lead to envy and both jealousy and envy will rotten a person's bones and can bring premature death (see Proverbs 14:30).

Conclusively, I am not sure to this day why Sam needed the $200 or where he got the car from he came to my house in, but a lot of his actions were questionable. Maybe the car belong to his disc jockey. Besides, at one point, when Sam was at my home I remember Sam stating to me to keep waiting. Waiting on what? You, or to date you, someone who is worried about losing a small amount of money invested in a concert, purchasing shoes or the latest fashions left and right, and has to ask me for money?

Also, I believe not only was Michelle jealous of me, but she was insecure too. She wanted something she saw as belonging to me and I was in her way of getting to it, Sam, so she needed to do something to remove me, something indecent and juvenile. Likewise, people should be careful when trying to come between people. For example, in a marriage. In some states in the United States, if a woman interferes in another woman's marriage or is a mistress she can be *sued* by the wife, so the wife can be compensated, for emotional damage per se.

Comparable to women behaving juvenile, leaders in firms do the same things to other leaders in firms they think are being considered for promotions, corner or center offices with large windows, and immense favor from executives they want. This happened to me when I worked at Wells Fargo Bank, N.A. and a similar event at Wells Fargo Financial. If you do not know or have not had first-hand experience, you need to know people do not like when you seem to be or *are* advancing. Instead of them working on advancing themselves they put their time and energy into hating you and trying to stop you from further advancement in whatever you're doing, which is impossible to stop when you're of The Christ. God will provide you hindsight, insight, and foresight about their behaviors and plans, Wisdom and strategies of how to work around them, and secret resources to keep moving forward while He plots vengeance and spiritual ambushes against them they did not see coming, letting people and organizations whom are *their enemies* come after them, suddenly.

Higher Education and Nicknames

One day Sam called me to chat as friends and told me he was in school again, currently taking a course, and received a B on a paper he wrote a few days ago. I congratulated him in a high praise manner and stated my baby got a B just to see what he would say. He laughed slightly in a shy way. I then came up with a nickname to call him and said again, he got a B on his paper. At that point he seemed to have gotten disgruntled about the new nickname, so I changed the conversation.

I later found out a few weeks or months later and after calling him an abbreviation of the new nickname in a text message, Sam did not like the name, asked me who I was referring to, and told me he did not like the name, indicative of he wanted me to stop. This was interesting to me seeming that he could create nicknames and use them, but I could not. Inclusive, he was not stupid, paid attention to things, and addressed issues up front when he was offended. The insights I gathered from the incident to make a mental note were two points: (a) he and people know when they play games and perform wrongdoing against others and (b) they do not like when games or wrongdoing is done to them.

Money, Best Friends, and Loyalty Agreement

As I described in chapter one, Sam's logo included the word loyalty. And at some point, during Sam and I's friendship I started receiving phone calls and text messages from an app telephone number. I spoke with Sam not long after and he stated some of the same things were happening to him. From Sam's conversation I gathered the problem happening to him was not as frequent as mine. I did not share with him the issue was taking place with me, but told him the incident that was occurring with him was weird.

> "I agreed and said I would do the same..."

Further, I refrained from telling Sam the same issue was happening to me because I was busy putting away groceries in my freezer, stuffing food in. While doing so, Sam sounded like he was looking at messages on his phone, stopped what he was doing and then asked me what I was doing because of the noise in the background. I advised him I was putting groceries into the freezer, stuffing the freezer because I bought too much frozen food due to not creating a shopping list beforehand and already had some of the item's I thought I did not have. He stated oh, okay and continued the conversation.

After a few minutes of chatting the conversation began to dull and the Holy Spirit (God) revealed to me a betrayal *from a friend* would occur sometime later. I spoke the information out of my mouth to Sam, but in a joking manner, stating, you know, we are close friends and friendship includes loyalty, so if you cheat on me I would not be happy, so make sure you do not cheat on me. Sam laughed, and I laughed as well, and he said okay. We both knew what I was talking about, but the conversation in my mind was also about the forthcoming betrayal, which I never thought anything about until the betrayal happened on valentine's day in the year 2010.

Henceforth, Sam and I made three agreements over time regarding money, best friends, and loyalty. Sam made a verbal financial agreement with me one day while I was in a McDonald's drive thru, ordering lunch, and speaking with him on the phone. We were discussing real estate, donating to non-profit foundations, and other business, with the majority of our conversation being about purchasing real estate investments, but not knowing enough information about certain real estate transactions. We were discussing real estate school, the cost, workshops close to where we lived, Sam's friend who was a real estate agent knowing information we were looking for, and attending classes together.

At the end of our conversation we discussed clients and contracts, briefly. Sam advised if he were to obtain a major deal or client, which would be income, he would share some of the increase, whether client, contact, deal, but particularly income, with me to help me advance a project, business idea, or business venture likely to bring a return on the investment, to get residual income rolling in from the concept, so to speak. I agreed and told him I would do the same for him because of a prior best friend agreement we made, and as long as we remained friends. Remaining friends does not mean we cease being friends for some reason and then become friends again, or never.

One day, on a Saturday I believe, when I was preparing to take a nap, I was speaking to The Lord about some things. Sam knew I spoke with God often and when he would call, to not interrupt me during our conversations, Sam always stated he would call me back later. Before my nap, God spoke to me and told me to make an agreement with Sam regarding becoming best friends. I called Sam and told him about the conversation God was having with me and Sam agreed to the friendship and did not ask any further questions.

Overall, I felt like I said everything God wanted me to say, I acknowledged this to God and after our conversation, from that day forward I moved on with assuming Sam did not forget about our agreement. At the present day, I believe God advised me of making the agreement because He knew the betrayal, *grief*, a healing process, teaching me about scandal, betrayers, and liars, total restoration, and a book to disseminate globally was coming in the years ahead to warn and liberate others, but also to use pain for my gain and new platforms. Just because someone is your friend, counterpart, acquaintance, associate, or close family member does not mean the person will not wrong you, in a major way.

The timing of when God approached me about writing a book on betrayal and how betrayal is connected to scandal and developed with lying came at the perfect time, during a season of conversations with colleagues around the world at two prominent institutions about diversity, ethics, and morality in organizations, leaders being ethical, ethics in various nations, and ethical problems in workplaces, to name a few. Conversations and workshops God kept delaying for a year and half, and I wondered why. The delay was necessary because I was growing during that time, and learning as I was still going through other betrayals. Now, I am able to think about our ethics conversations using a different lens, reflect on how what was said in the dialogues related to unethical situations I previously encountered, and better convey material and strategies in the book to you on how to overcome.

A Romantic Relationship?

Although I had quite a few conversations with Sam before about what kind of relationship we were in, I wanted to have the conversation with him again because confusion was in the air. Earlier in the book I conveyed Sam and I were friends, best friends after a while, yet during different times, conversations and physical touching was taking the acquaintance or whatever we had to a different level and needed to be cleared up. In the middle of another casual conversation Sam and I were having while I was driving from home from the city he lived in, we had the relationship conversation again. Again, I admit I wanted to date Sam, but I was not interested in a sexual relationship with him, something like that takes time to grow into, from a marriage standpoint.

The gist of the dialogue was Sam hearing me out and what I had to say about what was happening between us. I would like to keep the details about this part of the conversation confidential, but the conclusion of our talk was Sam asked me if I was interested in a romantic relationship with him because he was not interested in one with me at that time. I thought his decision was very interesting and Sam asking me if I was interested in a romantic relationship, in an absurd way, given all that occurred between us, but I assumed God was protecting me because I had already gotten Him involved in the ordeal and had conversations with Him about Sam and the matter. To conclude, regarding Sam's question, I was basically implying to him, do not play stupid, you know what I am discussing, we are both adults, speak on your feelings, and be truthful, yet I *chase* no one, especially not men (see Proverbs 18:22).

I've Always Been Interested in You; A Hidden Girlfriend

So, I can imagine what your reaction is going to be when I tell you one day when I was having another conversation with Sam after several additional romantic relationship gestures, him playing games, per se, I asked him what his gestures were all about and if he felt the same way about me that I did about him, from a physical attraction standpoint and if there could be a courtship in the future and he stated yes. Sam told me he had always been interested in me.

However, a few weeks or months after, during another conversation and while bringing the conversation to a close, I asked Sam if he wanted to do something together later that evening and Sam told me he could not because he was going to the movies with his girlfriend. You could imagine how shocked I was after our many conversations, which should have been about business instead. I dropped the conversation did not continue the charade and moved on with my evening. Still, I do know Sam is shy because we discussed it in the past when I asked him about it, but there is no excuse for all of the behaviors he displayed throughout our business relationship and then friendship, which signaled folly, scandal, betrayal, possible lying, and honestly, contingencies of psychosocial inadequacies. And there is more to the story.

A Colleagues' Wedding and A Valentine's Day Scandal

The day God approached me about helping individuals with some of their personal projects for free I was preparing to work in another city the following day. I agreed to what God was asking me although I did not know what kind of personal projects just yet, but knew He would let me know when the time came. The next, since the weather was good, sunny, and a great day to have lunch outside on my lunch break, I decided to buy lunch from a nearby deli and have lunch in the sun. After purchasing my meal and getting into my car to sit down one of my mobile phones rang and it was a friend of mine calling me to ask if I would help her with a personal project. I told her about what God had approached me about the day prior and she laughed and continued the conversation about how she knew she was supposed to call me.

    My friend has a cosmetic company and had the opportunity to provide her products and services to her friend requesting immediate help from her for her wedding. I knew my friend wanted my help and I did not mind for two reasons. First, I had already told God I would and could not rescind *my word* (see Psalm 15:4 and 1 Chronicles 17:16-27). Second, since the age of 19, I assisted friends (depending on what they wanted me to do) with their businesses and enterprise ideas by traveling around the nation of the United States with them to events, bridal conventions, large conferences, and universities to pursue ideologies they presented to me and the present wedding occasion was no different. So, I agreed to hear my friend out, decided to have lunch in my car, advised her I would be eating while she was talking, and asked her what her phone call was all about.

    My friend advised me that she knew I knew how to apply make-up to people's faces and first asked me if I would do this for her at a large event for a retail store she was now working with. I agreed and told her I would not charge her a fee to help her nor run the event through our corporation. Then I stated that was not about the wedding. She proceeded to state something happened with her friends' make-up artist, her wedding was a few days away, on valentine's day (February 14, 2010), the bridal party was flying in, and her friend was panicking about what to do about facials and applying make-up for the wedding, which the bridal party would also wear to the reception. Additionally, the majority, but not all, of the members of the bridal party did not know how to apply cosmetics.

While my friend was speaking, and I was eating I asked God if the wedding was the personal project and He agreed. I told my friend I would commit to doing make-up for the entire bridal party and the bride, for free because God told me too. My friend screamed with joy and stated she was glad because her friend told her the budget for the wedding was extremely tight, she still had to get her hair done and pay the hairstylist, and was not going to have any money left over for getting the bridal party's make up done, which she agreed to do. She also did not have any money in the budget to get her own make up done and was in a bind.

As a small compensation to show appreciation for my help my friend advised she would supply all of the products I needed, give me products for free (which she always did anyway with a lip gloss I love), drive to the city I lived in to pick me up to bring to the event, reception, and back home so I would not have to use gas, and ensure we would have our own private space at the luxury venue to work and change into our own wedding attire. Driving back home after the festivities was an option, but not mandatory since another friend of ours went to Louisiana to visit her family and son for months and left us in charge of one of her residential properties in a nearby city, which I went to on occasions to sleep whenever I was too tired to continue driving after any long day, and then work in her home office after being refreshed. Like after a parade our entertainment division participated in and I got sick during the event and had to bring my team to the property with me because they were riding with me. Yet, I was interested in returning home after the wedding events.

Overall, I agreed, was very happy to assist, and advised my friend I was heading home that afternoon and would begin gathering and preparing make-up kits I previously constructed, brought to, and our company used for some of our own large events, along with looking into the dress I planned to wear. I did not have a dress to wear and told my mother, and about the wedding. My mother told me about a store she knew of in a different city that had great clothes and interestingly sold dresses too. I eventually went to the store with her to look around and purchased the perfect dress I wanted.

A couple of days later I spoke with Sam and he advised me that he would be coming to my city for valentine's day. I did not plan anything and was just planning to see him and that was pretty much it, we were not dating. On valentine's day I spoke with Sam again and he assured me he would be on his way, that evening. I then told him about the wedding and how I confirmed with friends I would be attending, so I would not see him until late that night, but in the mean-time he should look into purchasing *some roses* for his mom for valentine's day. Sam agreed, and we ended the conversation because my friend was going to be arriving to pick me up to head to the wedding venue to find our rooms, attend the final rehearsal for the bridal party, set up our work room, including large portions of my friend's products for people to purchase, just in case they were interested. Likewise, Sam always did things late at night anyway after completing everything else he had to do during the day.

In my mind, I did not have much time to talk to Sam on the phone and thought I would tell Sam later to pick me up from the venue instead of coming straight to my house, which would allow us to get something to eat in the vicinity of the wedding venue and perhaps talk a bit. Then he could drive me home and head back home for the evening. On a previous trip to my home I told Sam since he lived three hours from me and it was dark during the night he could have stayed the night at my house, on the couch, and drove back in the morning to avoid danger or driving late at night. Then I quickly changed my mind, within a few seconds, and told him I would not want him to stay the night at my house because it was inappropriate altogether, personally and professionally. Therefore, the night of the wedding would be a long night, but we both would still have to retire for the night at our own homes.

On the way to the venue I told my friend I was going to tell Sam to pick me up from the venue, so she would not have to drive me back home and it would save her some gas. She was okay with the arrangement and advised me to let her know what time Sam was coming so she would know what time I was leaving the venue and to lock the room we were setting her products up in.

On the night of the wedding, the bride and one of her sisters cried while getting their make-up done and the sister stated she was crying because she felt so blessed to be getting star treatment and pampering, something she never had before. She had flown in to be with the bride from Ohio and stated she had an okay flight, but had been going through some adversity, had not told anyone, and the pampering was relief from stress. The bride cried because she felt blessed. I would have as well because the Word of God states God does not forget the prayers of the righteous, is attentive to their petitions, and answers when they call.

Also, the final rehearsal was absolutely wonderful, the wedding was astounding with a beautiful arrangement of the color red and roses everywhere and was one of the best weddings I attended thus far. I hope my family, friends, and colleagues do not mind me stating so! The reception was even better. Everyone who attended the wedding and reception stated so. The food was over the top fabulous and while the reception was going on the bride called me over to the wedding party table to express a sincere unforgettable heartfelt thank you about everything I had done for her, for free. She knew God had blessed her and would not forget the moment in time.

The bride also called up a handsome young man from Chicago who sat with my friend and I at our reception table, close to the buffet, which was what I liked, so I did not have to walk far from our table back and forth in heels. I loved being close to the deserts as well! The young man from Chicago was a poet and blogger who blogged and performed his poems via open mic in person, like I use to do/was infatuated with in undergraduate college. The young man paid for his own airfare and cab to get to the wedding, and did not charge the bride to be with her on her special day. I found this to be interesting and knew because the bride told everyone over the microphone and all I could say was *look at God*, such a phenomenal Heavenly Father.

I was blown away at how God came through for the bride and specifically *asked God to remember me* when my time comes. Remember how I obeyed when He asked, helped out for free, not just for the present wedding, but for various colleagues and the like regularly. I asked him to make provision for me to have what I desire on my wedding day, years in the future after I have built brands, gathered investments, and accomplished other things I want to do that are delineated on my *before I get married and have children list*. I believe when you behave appropriately towards God and other people, treating them respectfully, you have the right to approach God and ask Him for things you desire. I never understood how individuals who mistreat other people fix their mouths to ask God for anything, let alone try to speak to God after doing someone God loves dirty or just being unwelcoming to people in society in general.

Also, on the night of the wedding Sam never called me or text messaged me about arriving in my city. I did not hear from him all night and called and texted him a few times regarding his whereabouts, thinking he could have been in trouble. Based on past events of Sam getting arrested and encountering a flat tire, I was unsure of what to think. My friend asked me about Sam's arrival several times and I initially told her I was unsure and then told her about what was really going on. I eventually had to catch a ride home with my friend anyway and when I got home, texted Sam one last time to check on him.

Someone responded to my text message from his phone around 12:14am as if they were him, stating, "I am with my girlfriend". I later found out from Michelle on Facebook that Sam drove five hours minimum to the state she lived in to see and be with her for valentine's day. Sam and I lived in the same state, but to get to the state Michelle lived in Sam would have had to pass my city and house on the interstate. I found the news shocking, believed it, and also laughed, went to bed and decided to see what everything was about the next day, maybe. Also, I laughed until the next day when Michelle sent me a Facebook friend request to see photograph of her and Sam together and the *blow* of being a part of a scandal and betrayed began to settle into my heart. Sam showed me he was back stabber, sell-out, two-timer, supported my enemy, and double-crossed me.

Facebook Friend Requests

In corporations, when working with employees of the business the dynamics of teams is important for efficiency and is influenced by a variety of factors, such as the personal or private life factors of employees, environments, and leadership. Team dynamics are behaviors, attitudes, and outcomes. For instance, personal factors of members of teams that can impact the dynamics of the team is where disruptive members find ways to block accomplishments. Members of such teams seek to block the achievements of fellow team members, leaders, or the team altogether by frequently disagreeing with leadership or activities the organization participates in, by not participating in functions the team participates in, being exaggeratedly critical, and being inaptly outspoken.

> *"...people will enlist other individuals".*

The same tactics can apply to social media and firms that work with various individuals or independent contractors for events. People will enlist other individuals and tools as a strategy to prevent you for accomplishing something or moving forward in a direction, many times in a direction of or to secure something they desire that they think you possess the capability of getting to before them. I hope you follow what I am saying. The strategy is to stop you or a team, so *they* can inappropriately advance. God does not manipulate an advancement.

As Michelle sent me a friend request to my personal page on Facebook at the same time an unknown young lady did, who I later found out was possibly one of Michelle's friends or relatives (in this book I am referring to her as Michelle's cousin). I did not initially realize this was her tactic, scheme, or *trick*. Michelle needed other people to help her come against me with a scandal, so she could advance with her romantic relationship agenda with Sam, engaging in foolishness and *treachery* to be with a man, which is not proper courting (dating) etiquette for a woman in general nor a woman who claims to be of God (Christ). When considering courting someone, there are more aspects about the person that need to be known than the person's *external appearance*. Inclusive, God does not bless actions (or the procurement of a romantic relationship) done out of wrong motives or an impure heart (see Matthew 5:6, 8). A person with an impure heart has not truth in his or her inner being and whilst having a pure heart means your words, deeds, attitude, emotions, thoughts, and motives are pure (clean, uncontaminated, untainted, unadulterated, unpolluted) *and* align.

As Michelle sent me a friend request she text messaged me on my mobile phone at the same time, about calling me to start a casual conversation while I was riding in a vehicle with someone. The other person was driving, I was not, so I did not mind talking with Michelle on the phone briefly until we reached our destination. Michelle called because she wanted to know which church I attended because the church she was attending in the state she lived in at the time, two hours away from where I lived, had what she called *money hungry* pastors. I assumed she was talking about other monetary offerings pastors of churches sometimes request aside from normal tithes and offering.

However, I did not really comment on the money hungry pastor's accusations because offerings in churches are needed for different reasons and God operates or brings things to pass in life using a seed, time, and harvest principle. Money is seed and is needed to bring about a harvest in certain areas of life and is a strategy to pull things from spiritual stances into natural ones. I did answer Michelle's question though and told her about the church I attend, services offered, and briefly about how the organization has different ministries.

Additionally, Michelle and her cousin each sent me a friend request at the same time. As I was talking with her on the phone I found this to be strange and could only see the name of the requests at the time. Michelle and I then ended our phone conversation because we both had other engagements to attend to. When I disconnected the phone call and looked more closely at the friend requests from my mobile device to accept the friend requests, after accepting them, Michelle's cousin began sending me atrocious messages using vulgarity to bully me. She started negatively talking about my appearance and attacking me online in a foul manner, someone I did not know. I then looked at Michelle's Facebook page and saw her profile photograph was a photograph of her and Sam at what appeared to be dinner table in a restaurant with Sam's brother, Tim sitting next to them, and Michelle whispering in Sam's ear while smiling.

Michelle developed posts on her Facebook timeline about how she was going to a hotel for the weekend, for valentine's day. She engaged in postings about how the weekend was going to be fun and other commentary, postings staged for me to read. Different people commented on her postings by congratulating her and wanted to know who she was spending the weekend with, essentially asking about the new romantic relationship she portrayed to be in. The only thing the individuals commenting on her social media page did not know was how Michelle procured such a valentine's day weekend.

    After I briefly saw this information, I called Michelle back on the phone to discuss and clear up what she was trying to do. She laughingly did not take the conversation seriously and the discussion quickly ended. I immediately responded to the young lady who was sending foul messages on my Facebook platform and to some extent advised her that I did not know her, she did not know me, and I was not sure about what was going on with her, Michelle, and Sam; I mentioned Sam's real first name instead of band member stage name to see if she knew him. The young lady continued with lewd conversations that I sensed were demonically driven and for lack of a better words, extremely ghetto. I did not respond, so she stopped contacting me (see Proverbs 25:8 and Psalm 37:37). Psalm 37:37 discusses how there is a happy ending for a person who stays in peace.

    I also did not respond because I do not engage or entertain strife, confusion, distractions, or apparent competition. Jealousy, envy, confusion, and strife (see Colossians 3:12-14 in the Amplified Bible and at the end of this chapter) are linked and are attributes of wickedness and evil, Satan. I do not compete with people and you should not either. Further, no one can compete with me nor you because the Word of God relays we are all beautifully, fearfully, and wonderfully made, by God, and unique with our own set of finger prints with different life purposes, maybe connected, but distinct.

    Michelle eventually sent me a message on Facebook stating to *just move forward, from Sam* and with my life. She then asked if Sam comes to see me because he comes to see her and often? Michelle implied I should move on because Sam was with her and they were together, dating. I then asked Michelle if she slept (had sexual intercourse) with Sam, a question she did not answer and never responded to me online... or by phone ever again. The question was probably too personal, but considering the circumstances, our previous personal conversations, seeing the red flags of her betrayal to other women, and my personal and professional association with Sam, I had the right to ask. She could have not answered to keep the answer up in the air and me wondering since her implication of her and Sam dating was staged.

    The person I was in the car with at the time asked me what was happening. Although I did not know what to think and began immediately processing the incident from a spiritual standpoint in my mind, I told the person pieces of information, but not much to protect the incident and remain private until I found out more details. I filed the correspondence in a Facebook database to retrieve years later at an appointed time for a purposeful reason and telephoned my firm's vice president to advise what was happening.

    Henceforward, although I did not sign Michelle on with our entertainment division as an independent contractor during our first awards show with the production company discussed in this text, the action of deciding to wait to see what would happen with her was a good decision. My initial discernment about Michelle when I invited her to the first awards show and while observing hotel lobby gossip was accurate, even though I was not in Christ then like I am now.

    Not long after the valentine's day scandal and betrayal I immediately gathered all of Michelle's incident reports our organization was documenting on her and emailed her a termination letter. Michelle replied in an angry manner and told me *you are a real piece of work*. The statement was an improper way to act towards, speak to, and treat a person seeking to and providing you with opportunities, exposure to opportunities you did not seem to have prior to, giving you babysitter, financial, new vehicle, and personal life advice.

    The real question was, why was she so angry with me? Could the root of her anger be jealousy because she wanted something she thought was exclusive to me and wanted me out of the picture before what or who she wanted became exclusive? Historically and contemporarily the thought of such information intrigued me and was hilarious, but her bad decisions and actions needed to be disciplined. Maybe she was upset at the fact that she could not just do whatever she wanted to me, in the organization, nor get away with unjust behaviors, to rule and run *a show*, a travesty really. Vaguely, a part of the discipline was reputational repercussions of if other individuals or companies contacted our firm or me about her professional work, the truth would be told, and documented, to illustrate support as to why a good reference for her was not provided.

    Moreover, I saw my former pageant sister who attended Sam's Beale Street concert with me while out in the city one day and she knew by my demeanor something that was not good had happened to me and asked me about it. I told her, and her facial expression quickly turned from being excited to see me, to being curious about what was happening, to extreme disgust. She instantly asked, does not Michelle work for you? I stated yes. Too, I did not want to share what happened with too many people because I did not want to ruin Sam's reputation because I did not know what God had planned for his life, mine, or each of us business wise in the future and need to speak with God to clarify things, obtain strategy, and pray about the matter. In total, I only confided in approximately four individuals about the scandal and betrayal and carefully chose whom I told.

I made the decisions based on discernment and scriptures you should highly take into consideration and read, which are 1 Peter 4:8 (in interpersonal relationships, love covers a multitude of sins), John 13:34-35, *Matthew 18:15-17*, and James 5:16. Contemplatively, the valentine's day scandal was an abrupt ending to the mistreatment against me by various persons, inclusive of Sam and Michelle, and a kick start to telling Sam not to call me anymore. Also, I am extremely glad that when the scandal and betrayal occurred I was not in a romantic relationship with Sam, had not been courting him, was not married to him, was not in a five, 10, or 15-year marriage with him with several children and assets to result in ligation and child custody suits, nor tied up in any [major] business deals, contracts, real estate investments, community property, joint ventures, international agreements, business partnerships, charitable events, in the process of inviting Sam and his label to additional business functions, and more, resulting in more damage to me.

Still, if this or a similar type of scandal and betrayal happened to you and you are tied up in some of the business activities I listed, hope and options for recovery are available. God sees, hears, and will help you. Always remember people reap what they sow. And although I was not in a committed romantic relationship with Sam or any of the conditions I just mentioned, Sam, Tim, Michelle, or Michelle's cousin might be one day when a similar scandal or betrayal happens to them, to reap a greater pay back by God (see Proverbs 6:31).

SCRIPTURE REFERENCES

Biblical scriptures always help to put people, places, and things into perspective. Following, are scripture references, red flags, and lessons I learned as I reflected on the events described in chapter five:

- Sowing discord or separation among brethren is an abomination to the Lord. Anyone who deliberately formulates a scandal, participates in a betrayal, or lies to cause disharmony among people operate in sin and sin is always judged. Proverbs 6:16-19 says "These six things the Lord hates, indeed seven are an abomination to Him...A proud look [the spirit that makes one overestimate himself and underestimate others], a lying tongue, and hands that shed innocent blood...A heart that manufacturers wicked thoughts *and* plans, feet that are swift in running to evil...A false witness who breathes out lies [even under oath], and he who sows discord among his brethren".
- My perpetrators thought they were doing me wrong in the short or perhaps long run, but their actions were of The Kingdom of Sin and Unrighteousness (1 John 3:8), The Kingdom of Deception (Revelation 12:9), and individuals who practice lying are not of God, but Satan (John 8:44). The perpetrators actions were hurting them in the long-run because they *bound* themselves spiritually and *blocked* their own advancement in the natural, using sin. Furthermore, God equates liars to murders and John 8:44 backs up what I have told you throughout the book and states "You are of your father, the devil, and it is your will to

practice the lusts *and* gratify the desires [which are characteristics] of your father. He was a murderer from the beginning and does not stand in the truth, because there is no truth in him. When he speaks a falsehood, he speaks what is natural to him, for he is a liar [himself] and the father of lies *and* of all that is false".
- Sin is dangerous and can bring generational curses to your future generations (Deuteronomy 28:15 and Proverbs 3:33), will make life hard (Job 15: 20), can block your fellowship with God (1 John 1:6), has the ability to bring early death (Ecclesiastes 7:17), can cause disease and sickness (see John 5:5 and 14), can stop prayers from being answered (1 Peter 3:12), and causes success, prosperity, blessings, and provision to be withheld (see John 10:10 and Jeremiah 5:25).
- Deuteronomy 28:15 expounds "But if you will not obey the voice of the Lord your God, being watchful to do all His commandments and His statues which I command you this day, then all these curses shall come upon you and overtake you".
- When I think about how my culprits planned the scandal with Michelle being at the center of all of it, I recall what Proverbs 3:33 elucidates, "The wise shall inherit glory (all honor and good) but shame is the highest rank conferred on [self-confident] fools".
- Isaiah 32:6 is complimentary to Proverbs 3:33 and illustrates, "For the fool speaks folly and his mind plans iniquity: practicing profane ungodliness and speaking error concerning the Lord, leaving the craving of the hungry unsatisfied and causing the drink of the thirsty to fail". Folly means stupidity or lack of Wisdom. Both Wisdom and wisdom exist, and a capital W indicates God. Inclusive, the word thirsty is used in urban communities and references people

who are *desperate*, reckless, eager. Likewise, people behave how they think (Matthew 5:8), but should hunger and thirst after righteousness (Matthew 5:6).
- Job 15:20 explains "The wicked (*evil, corrupt*) man suffers with [self-inflicted] torment all his days, through all the years that are numbered *and* laid up for him, the oppressor". Wicked means the same as evil, malicious, sinful, very, extremely, desperate, unrighteous, evil, vicious, rotten, terrible, unethical, wild, and corrupt[9]. And malicious is related to the words envious, jealous, devious (tricks and schemes), and vindictive[10]. Vindictive people are interested in hurting people who seemingly cause problems for them[11].
- 1 John 1:6 posits "[So] if we say we are partakers together *and* enjoy fellowship with Him when we live *and* move *and* are walking about in darkness, we are [both] speaking falsely and do not live *and* practice the Truth [which the Gospel presents]".
- Ecclesiastes 7:17 contends "[Although all have sinned] be not wicked overmuch *or* willfully, neither be foolish-why should you die before your time"?

---

[9] Merriam-Webster, Inc. (2019). *Merriam-Webster dictionary app*. Retrieved from https://play.google.com/store/apps/details?id=com.merriamwebster

[10] Merriam-Webster, Inc. (2019). *Merriam-Webster dictionary app [thesaurus]*. Retrieved from
https://play.google.com/store/apps/details?id=com.merriamwebster

[11] Merriam-Webster, Inc. (2019). *Merriam-Webster dictionary app [thesaurus]*. Retrieved from
https://play.google.com/store/apps/details?id=com.merriamwebster

- John 5:5 and verse 14 illustrates "There was a certain man there who had suffered with a deep-seated *and* lingering disorder for thirty-eight years... Afterward, when Jesus found him in the temple, He said to him, See, you are well! Stop sinning or something worse may happen to you".
- 1 Peter 3:12 goes with Psalm 34: 12-16 and highlights "For the eyes of the Lord are upon the righteous (those who are upright and in right standing with God), and His ears are attentive to their prayer. But the face of the Lord is against those who practice evil [to oppose them, to frustrate, and defeat them]".
- Psalm 34:12-16 expounds "What man is he who desires life *and* longs for many days, that he may see good?... Keep your tongue from evil and your lips from speaking deceit...Depart from evil and do good; seek, inquire for, *and* crave peace and pursue (go after) it!... The eyes of the Lord are toward the [uncompromisingly] righteous and His ears are open to their cry...The face of the Lord is against those who do evil, to cut off the remembrance of them from the earth."
- John 10:10 claims "The thief comes only in order to steal and kill and destroy. I came that they may have and enjoy life, and have it in abundance (to the full, till it overflows)".
- Jeremiah 5:25 warrants "Your iniquities have turned these blessings away, and your sins have kept good [harvests] from you".
- I used to practice sin, like fornication, lying to my mother, and profanity here and there until I was age 25 when God began revealing the causes and consequences of sin and iniquity to me. Although I never lied to my father a day in my life (God rest his

spirit because my father transitioned into Heaven as I was facing many betrayals, adversities in life, and being lied on between 2008 and 2015), I lied to my mother on occasions, many times to protect my dreams. Still, lying was improper and I would only be able to see Gods blessings in my life if I stopped practicing sin, hence, a mixture of good and evil in my life and the words I spoke out of my mouth. Words are seeds people sow and can bring a harvest in their lives, whether for good or evil; you will *eat* your words, literally (see Proverbs 18:21). James 1:22 states "But be doers of the Word [obey the message], *and* not merely listeners to it, *betraying* yourselves [into *deception* by reasoning contrary to the Truth]" (emphasis on betraying and deception are my own, which I italicized because the scripture is profound and supplements the title of this book). In urban communities when individuals speak of betraying or deceiving yourself, the words "you're playing yourself" are used.

- When you have survived scandals, betrayals, and lies, God will give you double for your trouble, shame, or embarrassment. Other scriptures within disparate contexts highlight a thirty, sixty, one-hundred, seven-fold, and even a thousand-fold return. "And the Lord turned the captivity of Job *and* restored his fortunes, when he prayed for his friends; also, the Lord gave Job twice as much as he had before". -Job 42:10
- Genesis 50:20, one of my favorite scriptures proclaims, "As for you, you thought evil against me, but God meant it for good, to bring about that many people should be kept alive, as they are this day". The text is revealing our foe, enemies, haters, deceivers, or perpetrators may mean evil for your bad, but God will allow some evils because He means them for your

good: for promotion, development, and increase, increasing your womb spiritually, to birth new platforms, breaks, businesses, opportunities, and even friendships.
- God dislikes wicked thinking and evil imaginations. - Genesis 6:5-8 illustrates "The Lord saw that the wickedness of man was great in the earth, and that every imagination and intention of all human thinking was only evil continually... And the Lord regretted that He had made man on the earth, and He was grieved at heart... So, the Lord said, I will destroy, blot out, *and* wipe away mankind, whom I have created from the face of the ground-not only man, [but] the beasts and the creeping things and the birds of the air- for it grieves Me *and* makes Me regretful that I have made them...But Noah found grace (favor) in the eyes of the Lord".
- Someone who devises evil against a person, place, or thing has a wicked heart. Similarly, negative and inappropriate thoughts usually roam throughout a person's mind and come out of the person's mouth when improper information is housed in the person's wicked heart. Such individuals never do well in life, progress, and typically does not speak well of other people, including places, or things if you listen to what they talk about. For example, Proverbs 10:11 exemplifies "The mouth of the [uncompromisingly] righteous man is a well of life, but the mouth of the wicked conceals violence". The scripture is contending, out of the abundance of the heart the mouth speaks.
- To support Proverbs 10:11, Matthew 12:34 explains "You offspring of vipers! How can you speak good things when you are evil (wicked)? For out of the

fullness (the overflow, the superabundance) of the heart the mouth speaks". Each scripture is a strategy into understanding the type of people you deal with.
- You have learned throughout this book that evil individuals lie and are deceitful, which you need to know and understand as you go through life, engage in business, work with, and enter into relationships with people. In fact, evil people can be tremendously deceitful, which I discuss in other books after dealing with people *much worse* than the ones described herein. With some of the deceivers I have dealt with, only God was able to stir the course of the acquaintance, guide me step-by-step, day-by-day, and even hour-by-hour when dealing with the individuals to get me out of situations with them, *build me*, and conquer spiritual things only God could resolve, so I could forever be free in the natural. Evil people *say* one thing, but *do* something contrary to what they said. Psalm 28:3 clarifies this by explicating "Drag me not away with the wicked, with the workers of iniquity, who speak peace with their neighbors, but malice and mischief are in their hearts".
- Proverbs 24: 8-10 explains "He who plans to do evil will be called a mischief-maker... The plans of the foolish and the thought of foolishness are sin, and the scoffer is an abomination to men... If you faint in the day of adversity, your strength is small".
- Perpetrators will pretend like they do not know or remember what they did to you wrongfully by what a pastor friend of mine calls *playing dumb*. Both God and the betrayer know what transpired and God will repay. Proverbs 24:12 conveys, "If you [profess ignorance and] say, Behold, we did not know this, does not He Who weighs *and* ponders the heart and perceive *and*

consider it? And He Who guards your life, does not He know it? And shall not He render to [you and] every man according to his works".
- Instead of being concerned with doing wrong, be concerned about the One who judges wrongdoing and has the ability to place you in Heaven or hell; The One is Almighty, a power no foe can withstand (see Psalm 91:1).
- Do not entertain strife or confusion. Instead, know that you are as Colossians 3:13-14 states, "chosen by God for this new life of love, I dress in the wardrobe He picked out for me: compassion, kindness, humility, *quiet strength*, discipline. I am even-tempered, content with second place, quick to forgive an offense. I forgive as quickly and *completely* as the Master forgave me. And regardless of what else I put on, *I wear love*. It is my basic, *all-purpose* garment. *I never want to be without it*".

RED FLAGS
- The approach Michelle took to contact me out of the ordinary to ask me what church I went to and the simultaneous Facebook friend requests were red flags. I believe individuals can set their profile to only have people message them if they are on their friends list, which is what mine is set to. So, to finish carrying out her premeditated scandal, Michelle had to send me a friend request.
- I believe Michelle asked me which church I attend to bait me into having a friendly conversation with her while her and her cousin sent me Facebook friend requests to set up the remainder of the scandal, which was to curse me out online, have me see Michelle's profile photograph of her and Sam sitting at a

restaurant table together, and to read staged postings on her timeline about going away to a hotel for valentine's day weekend. Michelle needed to gain access to me to betray me and cause a scandal. The access point was talking about something associated with The Lord, who is someone she knows I am authentically about. However, Michelle's plan was of evil (Satanic initiated) to cause perpetual offenses to destroy me, my present and future work, and my connection with Sam. Satan knows offense causes blessings, life, and your spiritual growth (which impacts your natural life growth and success) to cease, including your access to and fellowship with God for Wisdom and guidance in any matter. Yet, *God will cause fools to be fooled, allow fools to be used by fools or each other,* and let foolish and devilish things people plotted and performed against you to work in your favor, largely.

- Sam asking me for $200, getting upset when I called him a nickname, but he could develop and call me a nickname whenever he wanted, telling me he had always been interested in me then stating he had a girlfriend were all red flags and catalyst to a more explosive inappropriate future event between us.

LESSONS LEARNED

- Love usually comes in several forms, Eros (sexual), phileo (friendship), storge (family), and agape (the God kind of unconditional love that is produced in someone's heart by God). I began to love Sam with friendship love and he *betrayed and breeched* a confidence we settled on, to share through a loyalty agreement. I recommend you do not talk too much, tell too soon, or trust or love too early. What is too

early? Ask God, depending upon the person and circumstance you are facing.
- A person can tell you one thing on the phone, via text message, or to your face, but be thinking, doing, or about to do another thing, contrary to what they led you to believe.
- I was briefly watching a television show one day and caught the last 10 to 15 minutes of the show where a woman on the show in her 60s stated behaviors men engage in are *romantic criminal* behaviors. Romantic criminal behaviors are where men flatter women and will be around them when they want, but seek to have their cake and eat it too, doing whatever they want. If a woman is not careful, romantic criminal men will *steal your money, time, and youth,* while convergently going out to restaurants with and dating other women. My mouth dropped opened as she said all of this, especially what romantic criminals steal because based on personal experience with men and observing circumstances some of my colleagues went through, it is true. Do not go back and forth with such people and pay close attention to their actions, which reveal a lot.
- People will hide sins they commit against someone else by not speaking about the issues for years, not apologizing to sincerely repent, and by secretly hoping the issue will go away. *You can run, but you cannot hide. Yet, you cannot successfully run either because God is omnipresent.* Furthermore, Proverbs 28:13 says he who covers his sin shall not prosper, only the person who admits to wrongdoing *and forsakes* the wrongdoing.
- People may hide sins and they may go unpunished by natural laws and legal systems, but not under Gods jurisdiction. God is Holy, and sin must be dealt with, whether now or later. Furthermore, Proverbs 28:14, 17-

18, 20 says he who hides his sin shall not go unpunished and will suddenly fall, into calamity, with no one to help. The same applies to a greedy person who hastens to be rich (see verse 20).
- People who work for you, visit your home, spend your money, eat food you bought for *your* corporate events and invited them to, and who form connections with persons in *your* network will betray you.
- When a scandal happens, usually someone is betrayed and lying is involved. Deception about a person, place, or thing was made to appear like something is was not. Both betrayal and lying regard being false and disloyal, while scandal is regards being shocked about a dishonorable incident, especially after some sort of honorable *agreement* was made.
- When people start to fall off of your life, God cuts them out of your life, or God asks you to remove the acquaintance, God is likely highly interested in blessing you with something new, fresh, innovative, and appropriate for your level in life, personally and professionally.
- Most of the people who scandalized, betrayed, and lied on me in my personal and professional life were not on my level, they were beneath me, subordinate. I find this to be interesting, but does not mean people on the same level in life as I would engage in similar misconduct.
- Subordinates in your workplace or life should not have the same access to you as non-subordinates. You need to restrict and reserve access to you for certain things, networks, colleagues, information, deals, acquaintances, and the like unless subordinates come up higher.

- You are not alone when perpetrators plot and attack you, even online. God is with you and other individuals likely have gone through similar or worse scandals and betrayals. Colleagues of mine have friends who were corporately betrayed in the workplace after being best friends with their betrayers for 30 years and working together professionally to build enterprises to go from private to initial public offering (IPO).
- The scandal and betrayal were an important pivotal point in my personal life, career, and organization and was one of the best things that happened to me to grow, develop, and gain incredible *ground* personally and professionally. For example, colleagues of mine describe ground this way: when you get into mudslinging battles with people, the battle will cause you to lose ground because you continuously bend down to pick up mud, curse words, or revengeful tactics to throw back at your counterparts. Doing so causes you to waste valuable time on people who are, in the long run, irrelevant to your purpose, assignment, and destiny in life. Irrelevant people are *distractions* to get you off track from recognizing or meeting meaningful, purposeful, and profitable relationships, business deals, networks, organizations, platforms, and divine connections by focusing on pettiness, offense, hurt, a scandal, or betrayal.
- When a person behaves badly, his or her morals or ethics that govern conduct, standards, values, and principles lived by need to be scrutinized.

CHAPTER KEY POINTS

- Scrutinize people such as business colleagues, friends, and casual acquaintances whom you have had problems within the past who ask you for money or want to come to your home.
- The luxury vehicle could have belonged to Sam's band disc jockey.
- Never ever mix business with pleasure under any circumstance, unless God tells you to. For instance, you and your husband work or pastor together. Lines still can be drawn regarding how to behave at work versus how to behave at home.
- The ordeals I was involved in with people throughout the book and especially in chapter five that were inappropriate was total and complete ridiculousness on my behalf. I should have never gotten wrapped up in any of the thoughtless and incongruent events on behalf of my organization and lifestyle as a business professional and leader, including publicly in Nashville with allowing physical touching. Never allow this.
- The people I dealt with were cold-blooded. I was also trying to provide individuals with opportunities who did not have the capacity nor character to receive or maintain the opportunities.
- Earlier, I suggested observing individuals for years because people will fake personalities, like they care and support you, take advantage of your kindness, and hide their true motives. Therefore, you have to be diligent with watching and assessing them for years, especially if you see red flags early on. Get to know people for a number of years before allowing them into your personal or professional space. Yet, the safest

thing to do is to ask God about people you come into contact with, for instance if you should befriend them or leave them where they are.
- If you are involved in similar matters, I advise you to get out of them, quickly, and keep reading. And if you were a victim of such matters, keep reading.

PART 3
GODS MASTER PLAN

CHAPTER SIX
Repositioning and New Perspectives

Cheer up! Do not be discouraged about the transgression people did to you, for many reasons, two I will provide for you here, which are Biblical strategies for increase. First, it was good that you were afflicted so you could draw closer to God and gain Wisdom to approach life and business from a different perspective, you were repositioned. Second, if you closely examine adversity you went through in life or people did to you, through Gods eyes, you will see how they increased instead of decreased you although perpetrator's agendas are to reduce and hurt you.

Culprits can push you towards increasing in a relationship with God, Wisdom, strategy, organizational change, corporate governance, changing the associations or company you keep, standards for business relationships and how you do business, how your company conducts business, and one of my favorites, in your finances. God will allow people who cause scandal and betrayal to increase you financially and will give you a strategies on how and reasons as to why. For instance, financial enhancement is a tool to use to gain access to greater opportunities (see Genesis 50:20).

Moreover, a betrayal or scandal is an opportunity to see people and places from a new perspective and to receive other new things from God. After the scandal, God will place people in your life who are not only genuinely interested in getting work done, but who are genuinely interested in you and your success in life. Such people will not *burden* you by constantly causing you problems, criticizing, looking down upon, or negatively talking about you to other people, including with incorrect information. The people God place in your life will be a *blessing*.

Using a nonfiction scenario, I can explain how culprits operate and will try to burden you, but will help you draw closer to God. As an example, people will try to or think they are controlling you or an outcome in your life by gaining access to something you once had, want, or they think you want and then start denying you access to something they have that they think you want, while you worry about the situation. For example, you lost your business do to a deal gone bad and in turn had a vehicle repossessed due to personal financial problems, a neighbor with a vehicle could have agreed to give you rides when needed, but might start denying you access if they see you becoming too successful without a vehicle although you still need one. Jealousy could be at the root, but control is too.

So, to gain access to your emotions, deliberately hurt you, and stop *some* of your progression since not *all* of your progression can be stopped, the neighbor will offer rides to another neighbor in front of you and lie to other people about your situation to make them look like the good neighbor and you a bad person. If you do not watch yourself, you will become discouraged, depressed, and angry about the situation, looking to the person to help you or faulting the person for not helping you by providing something you need, confirming their control and power by having something you do not, which is what usually culprits want. Access in some kind of way, to you, to retain *deliberate* control or power *over a situation* involving you so you do not advance, people do not get to know the real truth behind a bad situation happening to a good person, and your authentic recovery and restoration is delayed or forfeited if you handle discouragement the wrong way. You do not need to be around people like this. Ask God to open up a way for you or to give you Wisdom on how to get what you need.

Consider how this scenario can apply to some area of your life or business and reposition your thoughts using scriptures, your perspective about things so you do not get stuck, ask God for guidance and a recovery strategy from the situation, especially if you know people *think* they have gotten you good, gotten over on you, or their plan of demise worked, without numerous people knowing they planned they attack. See Psalm 28:3-5 in the Amplified Bible Version (AMP) and Psalm 36: 2-4 where people do not want the sin they committed to be found out and hated. One approach to repositioning your thoughts using scriptures is to repeat aloud that vengeance is The Lords and He will repay and now you qualify for double portion blessings, double for your trouble, as described in Job 42:10.

If someone caused your home to be foreclosed on because the embezzled money from your company or invested your firms finances into a known bad business deal, now you qualify for the restoration of two homes. Similarly, if someone repeatedly stole money from you to advance their own agenda and the person cares nothing about you, now you qualify for financial restoration, contracts larger than what you would normally qualify for with your skills and experience, and opportunities you do not have the skills and experience for, but can hire someone to do the work.

However, the double portion scripture is within reason. As an example, you cannot think if you lost a wife due to adultery with a friend you will now gain two wives. Adultery perpetrators have their own scriptures and judgements. Yet, God can provide you with a *better* wife.

A wife who is more successful, faithful, honest, and respectful, to be a blessing and not a burden to you.

God knows what *better* means for you or your organization, so let Him complete the choosing and arranging, not you because He created individuals and know who matches with who, why, and *based on their life's purposes*. This time around you can receive the wife God chose instead of a wife you chose and later had tremendous problems with. Plus, let God provide the better person *and* the judgement upon your offenders in His own way and timing.

A colleague of mine in higher education said something to the effect of people will discredit, dismiss, discount, disrespect, disapprove, disregard, and count you out...dissing you in just about every way a diss can occur. However, God will allow committers to think this for years and will then one day when they least expect it, remind them of the inappropriate situation and present judgement. And while they are under judgement you will be operating under and *open heaven* instead of brass heavens (see Deuteronomy 28:23), increasing.

To say the least, Michelle, Michelle's cousin, somewhat Sam, and Tim seemed to have moved on from the scandal and betrayal after some time, but God remembered the individualistic wrongdoings and the corporate scandal and betrayal that occurred. Over time, off and on, God had me document information from the scandal and betrayal and my perpetrator's lifestyles after the unjust incidents, which I later discovered was for the purpose of restructuring corporate governance materials in our organization, to provide you with strategies on how to survive a scandal, betrayal, and lies, whether in a workplace or not, how and why you should go to God from now on regarding all business decisions and acquaintances to protect yourself and companies, and to present you with material in the book. You need to protect yourself and firms *before* major increase happens, for instance, before amazing contracts are presented. Successfully surviving a scandal, betrayal, or lies can position you for increase because you will have the everything needed for the increase prepared, like contracts, governance documents, revised company policies, mission and vision statements, and the right team members. Offenders were just training ground if you look at the situation from a brighter side or situational lens.

The Holy Spirit and Documentation

Henceforth, I texted message Sam and emailed him an extensive letter about the valentine's day betrayal, told him about Michelle's topless photographs on her Facebook social media page with her ex-husband, and the content posted about going to the hotel for the weekend to see if he knew about the information. Sam did not respond to my long email to take a break as friends, tried to call and text me, but I did not answer because anyone could have been listening to our phone conversation or reading our text message conversation. So, I texted him telling him not to call me anymore and I would let him know when he could. I told him that nine to ten years ago. Yet, overall, I preferred an in-person conversation between the two of us.

Michelle's Facebook page was later pulled offline for a while or either deleted. I believe Michelle removed her personal Faccbook page and years later started a new personal page because I checked a couple of times to see how the betrayal would play out and to watch her, data I am glad I observed and is now useful for a book to warn and help people facing scandals, betrayals, and liars. She could have removed her page if similar subsequent events occurred, like the ones she did to me, or people found out about all of her unethical deeds.

Moreover, a long while after the valentine's day scandal and betrayal I perceived I should check Michelle's twitter social media to see briefly monitor the outcome of the scandal and betrayal. When I began reading Michelle's twitter timeline I noticed she was doing marketing and promotions for Sam's record label after I had discussed a Marketing Director position with her at our organization. The position at our firm came about because of her bringing up the conversation about wanting to obtain a bachelor's degree in marketing and conducting presentations at her university about our enterprise. You could imagine I found the information on social media to be odd and interesting.

I then wondered if Sam even knew the details of Michelle and I's professional relationship and the job position discussion, and originally thought he probably did not because Michelle hid information, lied a lot, was not trustworthy, was hypocritical, and our professional relationship was worked related. Or, Sam could have known because I do not know what their friendship was like or their conversations were about when I was not around. Then again, I found on three different occasions at the minimum, Sam was either working or conversing with colleagues I introduced him to.

> "...the birthing of the book you are reading".

After discovering the information on social media, I perceived I would review the social media here and there over the years to see where the online information would lead, to mentally document what was taking place and follow the patterns and behaviors of my perpetrators to see who was who and to recognize how people who commit scandal, betrayal, and lies act before, during, and after wrongdoing. As I discuss in chapter seven under the section ten years of observation, the outcome of mental documentation was the birthing of the book you are reading, new corporate governance materials and speaking topics, and content and presentations for corporations of all sizes. Individuals who encountered scandal, betrayal, and being lied on or to in personal relationships can benefit from the materials too. Furthermore, whenever I continue to observe something, someone, some place, or a geographical location, the Holy Spirit (God) typically wants me to document it or do something with it. In this case, one day when I was having a conversation with God about the betrayal, I told Him the content of the subject matter was so rich there was enough information to write a book. God then advised me a book is exactly what He was prompting me to write and I agreed.

Nassau, Bahamas Trip and Jet Skiing

Sam and Michelle were likely involved in a scandal and betrayal together against me because they do some of the same activities, like drinking alcoholic beverages. Michelle posted some photos on her social media with alcoholic beverages, for example bottles of brown liquor, with possibly rum, in the background. After careful observation over the years, Michelle tried to behave in a way Sam, and even other people would like, to accept her, by flaunting herself and liking sports. I am not into drinking and can remember on one occasion one of my awards show colleagues approaching me at an event during awards show week and stated he noticed I was not drinking for the evening when other business leaders were, yet I appear to stay focused on work our organization was appointed to complete.

For a different event outside of awards show week, I supported a recording artist at a few of his events he would invite me to. At one of the events I decided to see what all of the hype was about regarding alcoholic beverages and had a few sips of a drink. My colleagues watched me to see what my reaction would be. I did have a little bit of a hard time driving home that evening and a really bad time when I was five minutes away from my house. I had to pray to God to deliver me swiftly and He did, while promising to never engage in that type of behavior again, even if only minor.

When I got inside of my home, I texted Sam to tell him what I did and how I felt drunk. Prior to needing to get into bed to relax from the alcohol in my body, Sam texted me back and wanted to know more details about the evening and was excited about my drinking. I could not believe it, but his reaction signaled drinking alcoholic beverages and drunkenness was exhilarating and amused him. That was the last time I tried drinking and the last time I told Sam about something like that happening to me. I never had an alcoholic beverage conversation with him again.

On one of Sam's social media profiles during Sam and Michelle's trip to Nassau, Bahamas, Sam posted a photograph of him and Michelle on the beach together, laughing, with a caption discussing how he was drinking and his buddy (likely Michelle) added rum in his drink. What was interesting to me was the fact that both of them were together, on international territory, they met through me at one of our organization's corporate events, Michelle worked for me, Sam was my close friend, and I supported Sam's work, record label, and provided him with other business ideas and opportunities, including outside of his locality and previous work accomplishments.

Sam included a photograph on one of his social media of him jet skiing. A colleague of mine's husband advised other colleagues and I one day, without knowing any of our personal life situations, people will scandal, betray, and lie to you (his words was *do you dirty*) and then leave you for *dead*, but God will *bless* you instead. His commentary is correct. People will or will attempt to release a catastrophe in your life or corporation and then leave you and not look back to take responsibility for their actions, ask questions, check on you, dig deeper into what happened, see if you survived or recovered anything you may have lost, or if you healed, like the scandal never happened, moving forward to have a good time while you are stranded someone, seeking God for answers, or trying to repair any damage done to your business or reputation. Usually people do not look back until years later to research you to see where you are in life and what you are doing, and in a large number of cases find out they were wrong about the person they committed scandal and betrayal against, and lied on. Michelle also got the vacation she wanted (I discussed in chapter four) and initially asked me if I would go on, but did not mention to the Bahamas.

Self-Led Revenge or God's Vengeance?

Do not chase people, in general, nor for revenge. Anytime you start thinking about or pursuing self-led revenge on someone you are entering sin and Gods wrath, or vengeance could be poured out on you. God is Holy and *must* judge sin.

Likewise, do not pursue observation of individuals after a scandal, betrayal, or lie like I did unless there is a divine or legal purpose to do so. Otherwise, let people go and *spend* time (like money) on advancing. You do not have time to chase people to get revenge, even with them, or try to figure out why they did everything they did that was wrongful. Instead, you should be focused and your time should be spent on opening a new restaurant, a store, getting a new job, meeting perspective clients, flipping investment properties, or taking a free course to improve your business and bottom line. You can also be spending time with people who have your best interest. People who want to be or think you will chase them for revenge, an answer to what they did, or an apology are distractions and immature.

To demonstrate, based on a poll a colleague of my conducted on social media in 2013 regarding a question a fan of hers asked her to ask her supporters, approximately 33 respondents stated people who committed a wrongful act likely do not come forward to explain themselves or apologize because of the following reasons: the spirit of pride, ego, carelessness, immaturity, non-humility, no sound judgement, they are not as advanced in character as you are, do not respect you enough, they want to continue doing the wrong deed (sin) and are not ready to stop the charade, vulnerability and not being comfortable with showing the bad or admitting they were wrong (which is pride and pride is sin), may feel like the person they wronged will not take the explanation or apology the right way, might feel defeated, shame, or like they lost a good opportunity and forfeit the chance to start over with an explanation or apology, do not want to face rejection, the person they should explain or apologize to is a tough person and they are unsure of what type of response they will get, or the wrongdoer feels like you will never trust them again anyway. Pride is when a person is egocentric, conceited, arrogant, and only interested in themselves.

In my opinion, you do not need closure from anyone about anything, especially from people who do not have the capacity to do so, and correctly. Trust me when I say this, *God* will close a situation or ordeal and make sure you get your increase. If you chased after every person in your life who initiated scandal, betrayal, or a lie you would never get anything of real value achieved. Continue to work constructively. Every now and then you might look back at a perpetrator to remember how God delivered and restored you, but do not waste time on seeking an explanation, apology, or for the most part, self-led revenge.

Consider this, you are too expensive, you cost too much. In Gods eyes you are royalty, so do not lower your price, your standards or act out of character, getting on your betrayer's level to attempt to do to them what they did to you or greater, risking your God-led increase, better, opportunities, double, or restoration. A colleague of mine told me in the past, Bentley dealers do not try to figure out why every potential customer does not purchase a vehicle from them, everyone cannot afford a Bentley. Another colleague of mind told me years ago, do not have yourself nor be around people who have a $2.00 mindset, but want a $2 million-dollar lifestyle and remember, some people simply just cannot handle you, your success, or what you are about. This could explain why people do not apologize for wrongdoing, particularly if they find out they scandalized someone with a major role in a firm, which they did not realize before the scandal.

As I stated earlier, never let perpetrator's control you, an outcome *in your life*, or your emotions. Simply put, never let people who are lower than you control you. You have to have an ear to hear what I am saying to know I am not being boastful or belittling anyone. What I *am* saying is some adults act like toddlers and misbehave like toddlers. Parents do not let toddlers run their households. Alike, chief executive officers do not let babies control their firms. If you attempt self-led revenge, you put yourself into the immaturity, pride, toddler, and baby categories. Commit revenge into Gods hands. Based on personal experience, God does it bigger and better anyway, making a fool out of fools.

On another note, God will have people increase you when they are unaware. *Carefully reflect* on how betrayals throughout an entire friendship with a colleague occurred. Although wrongdoing was continuous you still should have learned something and improved in some way, whether personally or business wise.

Besides, offense is when someone hurts you. Hurt can be in the form of being lied to or on, manipulation, unmet expectations, feeling like you have been cheated or cheated on in some way, and deception to name a few. When you do not correctly handle hurt, shame, anger, unforgiveness, withdrawal, or revenge are some of the feelings than can result. Instead, seek to overcome evil with good, which is what I did, including not reliving the hurt because the scandal and betrayal did hurt me, from Sam's perspective. I expected Michelle to produce bad behavior because of my past experiences with her and knowing accusations others made against her about similar things she did to them. I was hurt by Sam's betrayal because I trusted him to be my friend, stand up for me when someone spoke negatively against me or plotted against me, and after everything I had done for him and his business, despite the red flags, and he still followed the way of a sly woman. However, I did not want to stay hurt long and immediately shifted my thinking from the hurt within 24 hours after the scandal and betrayal occurred because I knew it was not of God. Inclusive, the way you think will keep you from being successful personally and professionally, and your company from growing.

To be more specific, some of the critical key things I did to gather myself and not let self-led revenge control my thoughts (which would not have happened because I do not play I am going to get you back or chase after you for an explanation of why you did what you did games) or some other type of aggression were and for the reasons of:

1. Prayer
    a. *To keep my heart focused* on love instead of hatred to keep the way open in my life via my heart, attitude, actions, and mind (will, intellect, and emotions), to stay connected to God so blessings instead of curses could flow (see Philippians 1:9). Keep your heart clean and free of the clutter of sin, hatred, anger, resentment, folly, revenge, bitterness, jealous, envy, and the like, which Jesus terms *evil worthless fruit* (see Matthew 7:19-20), are signs of you are offended, and produce evil doing as God repeatedly discusses and warns against in the Word of God. Prayer using the Word of God and discussing situations with God helped me control my emotions and attitude and not let my emotions control me.
    b. *To hear God* provide me with insight about the situation and strategies and guidance about how He wanted me to respond to bring me

through the dilemma (see Psalms 85: 7-8; Luke 22: 31-32, and Proverbs 3:6).
   c. *To keep the way and communication open* between God and I for a public reward (e.g. a new platform, blessing, or opportunity) after everything was said and done (see Matthew 6:6).
   d. *To retain dominion or control* over the devil and not let him control me (see 1 Peter 5: 8-9). Satan needs people to sin (e.g. through strife, violence, their mouths, etc.) to control them. Like my emotions, I control hurt, pain, situations, and issues, they do not control me.
   e. *To receive* Gods divine protection (see Psalm 34:7), in general, and since I did not have comprehensive information to knowing all individuals involved in planning the scandal. People who scandalize usually plot in secret and then hide after the scandal goes public.
   f. *To get God fully involved* in the battle (see James 4:8) and leave the way open for God to assist me with succeeding in other areas of my life and our organizations (see John 15:5).
   g. To not get greatly worked up about the matter and *cease from anger* because anger will lead to revengeful thoughts and wanting to get even or commit evil (see Psalm 37:8).

2. Turn to and Read Gods Word (The Bible)
   a. To obtain strategies for business success after a scandal and betrayal (see Joshua 1:8).
   b. To renew my mind daily for a fresh perspective on how to behave, transform negative thoughts

the devil would try to send, and continue to succeed (see Romans 12:2).
c. To grow spiritually and keep Gods light shining in my life and not fall into error, mistakes, or act wrongfully (see 1 Peter 2:2 and Ephesians 4:14-15).
d. To keep communication between God and I open so He could answer prayers or petitions I had before Him about other things I wanted to accomplish in life or at work, including fulfilling promises He made to me personally and stated in His Word I could have (see 1 John 5:14 and 2 Corinthians 1:20).
e. To avoid being destroyed personally or professionally or my life purpose, assignment, destiny, and organization by acting out of character and at the level my perpetrators were acting on (see Hosea 4:6 and John 8:32).
f. To resist any temptation the devil would try to send me to return evil with evil (see Matthew 4:3-4), which is sin and would have caused me to be in bondage and held in captivity spiritually with no success or growth personally or professionally (see John 8:32). As I explicated before, sin can also result in iniquity, generating curses like financial, mental, family, and health struggles. Demotion instead of promotion in life, from God, can also result if you respond to scandal, betrayals, and liars (offenses) wrongfully. And to be blunt, you can also miss the Kingdom of God (Heaven) and go to hell when you transition. Sin can also bring early death which communities see time after time when gang

members retaliate against one another and is discussed below. Let God do the retaliating instead, against spiritual and natural adversaries.
g. Remember, like envy and jealousy, wrath or outrage can bring rottenness to a person's bones (see Proverbs 14:30), possibly even early death.

The bible comes in different versions, so select a version with wording you can understand, for instance, some people can understand the Amplified Bible Version (AMP) better than the King James Version (KJV). As I write this section of the text to you, I hear the Lord saying, if I would have responded to the scandal and betrayal, for example, through self-led revenge, to play the game, the situation would have gone a different way. Likely, in a way or with an outcome I later would have regretted. And consider this, I believe when you do not respond the way someone thought you would, the ball is now in your court to call and make shots, controlling you and your own response instead of letting foolishness or a foolish situation control you. After a length of time when your perpetrators remember you, what they did to you, and seek to find you, they will find you kept moving forward, working, building, growing, and developing ventures while they were playing, laughing, traveling and spending money they do not have, and thinking they got the best of you and did not. Move forward with God and work the situation in a fashion He would have you to work so you can have #TheLastLaugh.

Correspondingly, some people might try to justify self-led revenge, so they can feel better. For example, creating your own plan of how to get back at your enemies for what they did to you. Most of the time a physical fight, curse words, or a death takes place in these circumstances. A prime example are shootings happening throughout the United States in high schools, medical clinics, grocery stores, grocery store parking lots, on interstates and highways due to road rage, and most recently at a local municipality in Virginia Beach where a male employee was offended at work, left work to go get his gun, and returned to kill fellow employees.

Other than self-led revenge, some people who get hurt go into depressive states or kill themselves because the hurt along with other concealed or suppressed hurts they experienced is too much to bear. You never know what people are going through and a betrayer could possibly be held responsible for a suicide which is why planning scandals against people, manipulation, deception, high school games, and mistreating people should be avoided.

Even so, self-lead revenge never ends well. The outcome is typically an arrest, court case (which affects your money and flow), legal issues, and prison, resulting in the delay or destruction of your reputation, business, career, and life's purpose. Alike, court cases can affect families, communities, special needs children, and an individual could have issues with other people behind bars. Likewise, court issues produce hearings or proceedings, numerous paperwork to review and sign, voting rights problems, and division among friends, families, and future generations. And keep in mind, while you are engaged in arrest, court, or prison, your home, vehicle, assets, and so on will be vacant, need to be cared for, or sold because no successor is present, belongings you would need to purchase a second time if you are able to resolve legal matters. This happened to someone I knew a long time ago when I was 18, but the person was able to save *some* belongings from the apartment the individual was renting at the time because the person's father picked up the belongings, but not many belongings. The father did not have a car and could only take back to his home what he could carry on public bus transportation and everything else had to be thrown away.

Think about it, having your right to vote rescinded while being a convicted criminal serving a sentence would not be pleasing. Voting or advocacy rights can be negatively impacted at the local, county, state, or federal level with officials. Officials, whether they are corrupt or not will be making decisions about your well-being while you are incarcerated, your family, and more, without your input, including of telling you when you can eat, sleep, exercise, use the restroom, work, speak with friends, shower, and read a book. Since I have worked with organizations over the years to exonerate people who are wrongfully incarcerated, if you are currently incarcerated and are reading the book, use opposition to your advantage by having schedules you do not dictate work in your favor to discipline you. I would need to know your personal situation before I can provide an exact strategy, but you understand what I mean. However, as an example, if you are told to wake up at 6am, stop work at 3pm, and go to bed at 8pm, instead of complaining about it, think about how this could be your schedule in the future as a business owner, which you would be accustomed to because of discipline. Additionally, apply strategies, scriptures, and the like, mentioned in the entire book to your life going forward, starting immediately, to reposition yourself.

From an organizational standpoint, when considering voting and advocacy, not being able to voice your concerns about healthcare and corporate income taxes (at the state and federal level) is critical. Corporate income tax rates enormously impact your business, employees on many levels, and your personal income. Self-led revenge against people who have nothing to do with your destiny is a waste of time and money, hindering your wealth and the manifestation of legacy, a powerful brand, and a global enterprise, if applicable. Revenge against one or a few incompetent people, when millions of customers are waiting on your organization to bring a revolutionary technology device to market to improve lives, cure cancer or Alzheimer's disease, or increase other companies' proficiencies and efficiencies is a waste of energy and resources, like using the sleep you got last night to spend an hour plotting revenge and enlisting your own computer, money, friends, or company as resources to do so. Gang members find themselves in the outcomes listed because they immediately operate from feelings and emotions, let hurt or offended emotions and feelings turn into aggression or anger, and seek to get revenge to prove no one will *disrespect* them when really, perpetrators disrespect themselves because the disrespect likely falls into a category of sin and sin can bring curses. Remember?

So, the keys to stopping yourself from being led by your feelings or emotions to take revenge matters into your own hands are: have a relationship with God/Christ *before* trauma strikes, immediately go to God when the dilemma surfaces, and having the Word of God established in you so the Word can quickly work on your behalf when adversity hits. As previously briefly mentioned, but in a different way, each of these techniques were how I *quickly* overcame, gathered my thoughts, and came up with a plan as to how not to react to the betrayal. Discernment was in place as well to know what God was saying. Further, wrongful actions people engage in and then move on like nothing occurred will eventually come face to face with the obscurity in the future. Bad behaviors do catch up with people. And as a recommendation to leaders of organizations, when you cannot get natural laws involved in scandals or betrayals that happened to you, get God involved and His spiritual laws.

Spiritual laws exist, including financial spiritual laws. If you mistreat others, mishandle money, or seek to inappropriately handle other individual's finances, financial curses can result and cause financial advancement issues. God will repay. Just make sure you do not repay because God does not take pleasure in contempt (disrespect) or taking his Word condescendingly, you will reap what you sow (Galatians 6:7-9).

I remembered you reap what you sow when thinking about what a former colleague of mine did when I, as the chairperson of the board of directors and chair of the nominating and governance committee of a prominent institution, appointed her to the board to be the chairperson of an events committee, secretary of the board, and led person at company annual events to practice speaking in front of numerous people, on a microphone (which she extremely terrible at). Too, I appointed her as lead person to practice speaking in front of people because it was in my best interest. I was frequently going to a hospital in a city where events were held to visit my father, who was dying, which my former colleague knew and expressed sympathy to me. The individual later called special meetings at the institution without my knowledge and did not invite me. She also set up a final special meeting to have me removed from my chairperson position and the board entirely.

I was going through all of this about a year to four years after the valentine's day scandal with Michelle, Sam, and Tim. Inclusive, my former colleague who had me removed from the board wanted my chairperson of the board position. After research and attempting to speak with each person of the board I appointed to various positions, committees, and sub-committees, I later found my former colleague secured my chair position by working with staff of the organization we sat on the board of. She was in photographs at events, laughing and talking with people like nothing happened. I also agreed to mentor one of the board members (who I appointed) because she asked me, helped her become an accountant, a part of a professional association, consider opening her own practice, and let her use me as an industry reference. She then betrayed me, did not show up to board members, ignored my phone calls and emails, and more.

After the board betrayal and the member who I mentored personal betrayal, nearly one year after, she tried to email and call me for the next three to six months because she knew she had wronged me, and I was [possibly] a door into her next level of success or opportunity. You could say she came to her senses or she spoke with someone and the person told her about her wrongful actions and how I helped her advance. I ignored her, had all of her correspondences and phone calls blocked so she could never contact me again, and moved on.

The end result of the matter was none of the individuals who participated in the scandal and betrayal, knowingly or unknowingly stayed on the board long after I was removed, and staff persons of the institution moved to different companies in new job positions. One of the staff persons involved, who worked in a prominent position in the company tried to reconcile with me about a year after the scandal and betrayal with a colleague of ours in the Seattle region of the entity who worked with the staff member to bring my idea of regional leadership conferences for the organization to fruition.

Overall, I believe my former colleague lied on me or about something I was connected to and enlisted and *convinced* the rest of the board members to vote on removing me. No one provided me with a straightforward answer as to why the decision was made to vote me off of the board which was suspicious, seemed provoked by jealousy, but could have had something to do with the bylaws of the Board. I also gave my former colleague too many opportunities, positions, and power in too many areas, too soon and should have let her *work* her way into the opportunities *over time*.

I did not respond to anyone who tried to reconcile with me, but had forgiven them instantly when the scandal and betrayal occurred so I could move forward and not be stagnant in life, continuing to grow. I moved on to bigger and better opportunities. The betrayal happened at the right moment, when I was trying to decide on whether or not if I should step down from the board and pursue another opportunity that was forthcoming.

Since then, for all current board seats I occupy as a chair and will occupy I carefully review and revise bylaws provisions and clauses, to prevent scandals, betrayals, and injustice against anyone, including myself. Careful reviews and revisions are made to ensure people are not given too much power, power they should not be given for the position they are appointed to, and power within a certain area too soon because persons who engage in scandal, betrayal, and deception mean to. They deliberately plan to disrupt or try to take over a persons' life, business, venture, role, or connection with someone. Not responding was the best course of action, to protect myself spiritually and possibly legally. I did not pursue self-led revenge, but did ensure my former colleague did not receive any information from me, my hard work, or board office I built for the region we worked in, and that she had to start her chairperson role from scratch, as much as possible. The board betrayal confirmed to me people will want your position in organizations and do not even know what they are doing, do not have the years of experience you have for the company and position, nor the resources or Wisdom to *maintain* the position once they unjustly secure it.

Beef Up Security in Your Life and Organizations
In chapter five I briefly discussed subordinates in your workplace or personal life should not have the same access to you as non-subordinates. Restrict access to you for certain things, networks, colleagues, information, partnerships, contracts, deals, acquaintances, and the like. By access, I am referring to contact information, conversations, watching the company you, and even who as far as who you invite into and entertain in your home. I now only work with a limited number of persons and employees, limit my involvement and job responsibilities outside of the office in the field, and restrict access to me by limiting access to reasonable *and a certain number* of people. The same applies to your organization to scrutinize and limit your firm's connection to only positive, applicable, and quality networks, projects, and partnerships that will enhance the business and not attempt to cause disruption. Restriction must be done so you only give your time to credible persons and reduce or

avoid altogether the opportunity to waste time on people, places, events, or things where the time can be best utilized on more productive projects, firms, and individuals.

    Beefing up the level of security, or oversight per se, in your corporation is necessary to protect shareholders and internal and external stakeholder's interests. To explain, I have observed people who tried to *steal* large amounts of money from other individuals, right under their noses, using deception, manipulation, and successors the persons named, opened and transferred monetary funds between various bank accounts, befriended the individuals with the intention of stealing finances, and worked for years on draining six figure compensation pools the perpetrator was seeking. The culprit went as far as to begin studying and understanding successors of the finances roles and legal documents to locate an opening in agreements to insert their name to *legally* gain access to the finances.

    Aside from limiting your actions with certain individuals inside and outside of your workplace, I highly recommend the following: chose responsibility delegation wisely, create or revise business documents to protect your enterprise from the legal and non-legal ramifications of scandal, betrayal, and lies, begin to increase the ethical culture of the administration, and attract people to the organization who will comply. Corporate governance and ethics instruments should also be used. Some instruments are the documents of adopting a Code of Ethics or Statement of Ethics with disciplinary rules embedded, a company Code of Conduct, Vision and Values Statement, Supplier Code of Conduct, Unfair, Deceptive, or Abusive Acts or Practices Policy, Human Rights Statement, Conflicts of Interest and Outside Activities Policy, Gifts and Entertainment Policy, Human Resources Guide and

Handbook, Unethical Activities Reporting and Nonretaliation Policy, and Corporate Governance Plan or Guidelines with you abiding by each of the policies too. If you are self-employed and only have a few employees or own a small business, four documents you should start with until you become larger are Finance and Accounting, Audit, and Executive Compensation Committee Charters for board of director's committees and a company Code of Ethics. Hence, you should have a board of directors and three board committees.

Any of the documents listed herein should be disseminated in meetings, trainings, orientations, or the similar times of gathering, including to board directors. The documents should align with local and federal laws and regulations and the objectives, short and long-term interests, values, and policies of the company. Large companies, whether public or private, should have a full and complete ethics and compliance program with an appointed Ethics Oversight Group to locate the red flags leading to misconduct, unethical, or unlawful practices. Having ethics procedures or a compliance program is not only advantageous for protecting an administration from scandal, betrayal, and liars, but to retain personnel, clients, partnerships, friendships, acquaintances, long-term market share and valuation, and reputation. If a major unethical event occurred in your entity, you could hire a human resources, management, or ethics consulting firm that specializes in or has risk analysis, reputation repair and management, crisis strategy and planning, litigation support, expert witness testimony, and reputation rebuilding services, to name a few. Overall, carefully planned, crated, and disseminated company standards, statements, policies, codes, charters, and or procedures need to be developed to recognize and prevent misconduct and to let deceivers know *you and your organization mean business*.

When disseminating the information to board members, ensure a meeting is set aside to comprehensively go through the documents because as I was writing this book I reviewed the board documents I redeveloped and amended from the board I sat on when I was betrayed by a member I bring in I told you about in chapter three. Although the documents stated certain procedures were to be followed for certain board positions, the main betrayer did not adhere to protocol because she did not fully read the documents. I recognized this when I reviewed the documents and reflected on her patterns of behavior and conversation's I had with her before the betrayal.

God-led Business Decisions

To be clear, concise, and straight to the point, assessing individual's patterns of character and behaviors, and producing institutional statements, policies, and codes are great for legal and ethical corporate culture reasons, but to accurately know if a person has a negative agenda when you encounter them, so you can avoid scandal, betrayal, and lies leading to catastrophe, involve God in *every* business decision you or your company makes. God-led business decisions should happen all of the time and not just some of the time. Based on personal experience, before and greatly after the valentine's day scandal after my relationship with God became extremely fine-tuned, God will warn you either years, months, weeks, days, and hours in advance of a bad acquaintance, future business relationship, or devious person. I have also encountered some incidents where He warned me when I had just met someone, while in their presence.

The benefits to applying God-led business decisions are innumerable, but some are God will tell you when to amend business documents, in advance, to protect you and your organization, will distract, delay, or altogether ruin a bad business deal someone or some organization plans to present to you to take advantage of you, and will ensure monetary negotiations are adequate and you do not get cheated and receive the short end of a contract. I have experienced each.

To be bluntly honest, I cannot do business or life without God. If God says no to me about someone, some place, or a business decision, I do not make the decision and retreat from all association with the decision including the persons and organizations connected to the business decision, if God tells me to. I also know that if I do not, God loves me so much and has invested a lot in me to where he will either forcefully remove the deal or acquaintance or allow some sort of initial detriment to occur to save me from further damage. I have gone through my share of such experiences and am not interested in going through more. So, I heed red flags now and obey God speedily.

SCRIPTURE REFERENCES

Biblical scriptures always help to put people, places, and things into perspective. Following, are scripture references, red flags, and lessons I learned as I reflect on the events highlighted in chapter six:

- Wisdom and knowledge are dissimilar (see Proverbs 24:3-4), yet both are significant. People who operate absent of knowledge or Gods Wisdom are spiritually blind and usually encounter natural life problems that could be avoided by listening to Wisdom to follow strategic guidance and direction. Wisdom helps you steer clear of sin, mistakes, or facing an ultimate destruction. If an individual wants to follow someone who lacks Wisdom because the route with them seems pleasurable, let them go. Matthew 15:14 explicates "Let them alone *and* disregard them; they are blind guides *and* teachers. And if a blind man leads a blind man, both will fall into a ditch".

- Hosea 4:6 proclaims "My people are destroyed for lack of knowledge; because you [the priestly nation] have rejected knowledge, I will also reject you that you shall be no priest to Me; seeing you have forgotten the law of your God. I will also forget your children".
- Even if you are scandalized, betrayed, or lied on God promises to deliver whoever is of Him. Psalms 34:19 postulates "Many are the afflictions of the righteous, but the Lord delivers us out of them all".
- Regarding contemplating pursuing self-led revenge, Ecclesiastes 7:9 expounds "Do not be quick in spirit to be angry *or* vexed, for anger *and* vexation lodge in the bosom of fools".
- To help you not take situations into your own hands and pursue self-led revenge recall Hebrews 12:14, which states to "Strive to live in peace with everybody *and* pursue that consecration and holiness without which no one will [ever] see the Lord".
- If you take matters into your own hands and do not do things God's way, unfavorable actions, including legal, can occur. When you rest, God works. If you walk in love, God will be with you and people will recognize you are of God. First John 4:12 highlights "No man has at any time [yet] seen God. But if we love one another, God abides (lives in and remains) in us and His love (that love which is essentially His) is brought to

completion (to its full maturity, runs its full course, is perfected) in us"!
- It is important to keep the way open for Gods wrath and keep your heart, mind, and emotions clean and free from sin or revengeful thoughts because out of your heart flows either issues in life or promotions from God (see Proverbs 4:23).
- It is also critical for you to keep your heart clean and not engage in self-led revenge because if evildoers boast about the wrongdoing they committed for revenge, their light will eventually be put out, cut off within the short time to come (see Psalm 37:1-2, 8-10). The scriptures also contends, do not be envious of evildoers, they will be cut off and their light put out. God is saying do not be envious of evildoers by thinking they are getting away with bad behaviors with no punishment; culprits wrongdoing have an expiration date and their time of judgement is coming.

RED FLAGS
- After careful observation, Michelle's original intentions with Sam come into manifestation. So, her patterns of character and behavior were accurate.
- People will tell and then show you who they are if you listen attentively and observe.
- I gave people too much access to me and our firm too soon.

LESSONS LEARNED
- Do not worry about anything nor anyone. Considering things and money I had given to people mentioned throughout this book and in chapters five and six, I learned over the years and through conversations with God that *God will allow you to recover what you lost*, what people stole from you, and from bad investments you

made, whether monetarily or relationship wise. Relationships are associations and include friendships.
- Restrict or limit access to you and your business for quality, meaningful, positive, and appropriate relationships, projects, partnerships, and associations.
- Enforce personal standards and business policies upfront with people to reduce future scandals and betrayals.

CHAPTER KEY POINTS

- Do not let people or situations control you by what is done to you, wrongfully. Be concerned about what God is doing *for* you and *through* you. Remain business minded and focused.
- The following statement may sound condescending , but is necessary to state so you can continue succeeding and advancing in life or business: do not sweat small stuff or *small people*. Small stuff and people are disruptive and do not understand or recognize big people, big things, big deals, big life purposes, and big dreams. The things small people focus on are small and small people do not possess the *mental capacity* to house what big people or potentially big people who are in transition to being big think. Small people's minds cannot handle the greatness big people house, ponder, and began to implement.
- Small people's and big people's thinking are totally divergent, on two different teams, and on two unlike dimensions. I know, because I use to think and behave small until God forcefully cut people, places, and things out of my life to get me on a better path. He also reconstructed my thought life through seasons of isolation of only being with Him. The isolation and reconstruction were highly needed, so I could operate

in the big purpose and leadership mantle God placed on my life. Isolated seasons of only focusing on God were about sleeping, eating, working, no social connections or outings, only having conversations with God, and doing the same thing for the next day to change my perspectives about people, places, things, and business decisions.

- If God calls you into a season or seasons of isolation, do not fight Him about it, but embrace the isolation, which may be difficult at first because you are not used to it, but will be highly beneficial in the long run. Isolation grows you for the better like you would have never thought and is necessary for your next levels of business decisions and success.
- Always *keep the way open*, the connection between you and God, by not participating in drunkenness. By drunkenness I am referring to being drunk or more interested in alcoholic beverages than business, meeting the right people or connections, opportunities, and your destiny. For example, always be sober minded, alert, and ready to hear from God, to receive advise, ideas, strategic direction, and insight about deals, opportunities, life, and progress, whether personally or professionally related. Drunkenness will clothe a man with rags (see Proverbs 23:21) and is a trick of the devil to produce clouded judgement in a person so she or he cannot appropriately discern situations or receive wisdom, innovative ideas, financial increase, or insight from God about concerns. For instance, which geographical location to live or open a business in. Similarly, Proverbs 22:15 states the following to a certain extent: drunkenness is not cool or cute, but childish, ignorant, and foolish.

- God put in my spirit, tell people, *instead of catching court cases, catch flights*. Private flights hit my spirit and exude luxury, class, and status. I told Him, Father God, you make me laugh, but what He said is true. Do something meaningful and designed to bring you increase from scandals, betrayals, and lies instead of responding to them negatively to disrupt what God is doing or is about to do in your life. Fly high instead of stooping low to someone else's level to try to get back at them for something he or she did to you, cowardly. Getting people back is not your place, but God's.

CHAPTER SEVEN
Treading Carefully

Ethical awareness in an organization must be created and can be achieved through various forms. Similarly, when you belong to Christ, never let a perpetrator, vicious, or corrupt person, devil, scandal, betrayal, or lie, control, limit, overcome, or defeat you. You have access to too much power in God to be indefinitely taken advantage of, defeated, scandalized, or betrayed then left for dead.

People know what they are doing, when they are doing right or wrong. For instance, Sam posted on his Twitter timeline as I was completing this book and stated he was going to send his mom some flowers, but he knows her and sent her some money instead. The flowers could have been for her birthday or another occasion, yet the key observation is the comparison of him sending flowers then, but practically ignoring my suggestion of purchasing his mother roses for valentine's day and driving to the state Michelle lived in instead. To learn more about his behaviors and everything I went through with him and the culprits who came against me he was affiliated with, so I would not make assumptions, I decided to observe their actions over time to learn more. I did not have an observation time-line set of when to start and when to stop, I decided to be led by God and He would let me know when the research was complete and what to do next. Inclusive, I would know when the research and process was finished when God revealed to Sam how Michelle plotted against me and wronged me, and he was involved without knowing things about her I knew.

Ten Years of Periodic Observation

Along with the information I discussed in the Holy Spirit and documentation section in chapter six, I engaged in the documentation for 10 years to *observe* my perpetrator's behaviors and *learn* from them. I conveyed on previous occasions in this book that sometimes you find out who people truly are when you first meet, at other times it may take 30, 60, or 90 days, and in some instances, three, five, or more years. The time-frames can vary, but people who behave inappropriately and have abusive intents possess similar patterns of behavior and timeframes in when they reveal who they realistically are. For instance, during the 10 years of research, via observation per se, God also had me observe several other individuals and document my experiences with them and their corrupt behaviors. I identified although you might not realize who a person really is early on with one individual, but may realize who a person is in another case, every problematic person displays warning signs.

After scandals, betrayals, and lies are completed and exposed, individuals who know they did wrong and have even the slightest bit of conscious that is not seared have certain behaviors too, like trying to contact the person they wronged, in the wrong way, without just being an adult by repenting and saying 'you know what I was wrong, I lied, I engaged in the actions inappropriately, was childish, and ask you for your forgiveness'. What I do have a problem with is when a person claims to be of the Christ, holy, or some sort of individual who is interested in empowering others, but who feels no remorse about the corruption done, which they planned and carried out. I have issues with people who are not immediately remorseful, who take a long time (years) to be remorseful, and who only become remorseful after a something traumatic or similar scandal happens to them.

Do not ever become reacquainted with someone whom God let you hear the conversation He had with the person who did you wrong and told the person how the wrongdoing came about, with whom, how they were wrong about you, and then the person contacts the individuals whom God spoke to him or her about regarding the situation, but no one ever seeks to contact or reconcile with you. After ten years, the same way they located one another's contact information to discuss how God spoke to them about their wrongdoing is the same way they can find out where you are to authentically repent, whether at the 10-year mark or not, but it should not take that long. Small children know when they have done wrong and immediately repent and say they are sorry because they know if they do not, a time out is coming next. Adults who are of God are the same way and know non-repentance can have immediate life as well as eternity consequences.

Yet, if repentance does take long or never occurs it could be because, as some people say in their communities or cultures, is because the person or persons are *salty* about how things turned out. They thought they were doing you in, but found out their nasty schemes worked in your favor, which is appropriate because God will make a fool out of fools and publicly expose people after a while of non-repentance, even if they *do* claim to be of Him. Psalm 86: 17 in the Amplified Bible states "show me a sign of [Your evident] goodwill *and* favor, that those who hate me may see it and be put to shame, because You, Lord, [will show Your approval of me when You] help and comfort me".

Unknown Email Sender & Photographs

Do not allow people, who have scandalized, betrayed, lied to, or lied on you, and after extensive research seem to not have done much with their lives, to just waltz back into your life once they find out about your continual progression and success in life, figuring out how they were wrong about you. Inclusive, you have likely grown and advanced over the years after hard work or because of the scandal, betrayal, or life if you handled them appropriately, and as a result are likely to be on a different level mentally, academically, professionally, socially, and economically from your betrayals. So, allowing a future association with him or her would naturally be uneven, unfitting, and skewed, unless God said to, *which He rarely does*, but usually does not and there must be a purpose for the connection. Deserted parents who find out about their children becoming sports athletes and signing major contracts with household brands attempt this and it looks skeptical.

Furthermore, people who participated in or knew about the planning of a scandal, betrayal, or lie are just as guilty as the individuals who conceptualized and performed the wrongdoing and do not deserve to come into your life to be on the same playing field personally or professionally after you have been working, growing, developing, building enterprises, planting, and harvesting. Each takes going through hardship, lack of sleep, and years of excruciating sacrifice…spiritually bleeding while leading, toiling, growing, healing, advancing, recovering, and moving into something better with people who are and are in networks that are greater than you were previously involved. The wrongdoing and deception worked against perpetrators, but in your favor, if you know it. Amos 3:3 contends, how can two walk together except they agree? So, pay attention to what happens around you and do not be distracted by people, places, or things in life. Do not be so naïve to where you overlook or choose not to remember the damage or hell a scandal, betrayer, or liar put you through.

After researching Sam's Instagram social media, his postings and commentary revealed his *primitive interests* of drinking alcohol, smoking in a club, purchasing sneakers or games, food, a few photographs of his family members, and...Michelle. There is no indication of detailed interests alike mine or the direction I am headed in personally or professionally, only a previous few about real estate and health foods. Yet, there is a saying that goes, 'you are what you eat'. The saying can apply to, 'you are who you hang around or what you entertain'. I am not interested in entertaining a social media filled with games, shoes, smoking, or drinking, unless there is a serious business reason for the shoes and games.

For pairs of shoes costing $50 or $52 at the minimum, I can turn the cost of one pair of shoes into a business idea to reap a global profit with yield coming in from numerous nations. The same scenario applies to individuals who want to be associated with you or your organization, but spend finances on one home, car, hair appointment, or outfit when a venture could have been funded to produce residual revenue. To be honest, nearly every time I see someone on a social media platform, in my immediate or extended family, or in distinct organizations engage in such behaviors I immediately calculate i my mind what I could have done business wise (even within a non-profit organizations (NPOs) social impact investment) with the smallest amount of money they spent on the endeavor. Just being associated with someone can influence your reputation, whether for good or bad.

Each scenario abovementioned reminds me of social media posts people post on Facebook. To illustrate, 300 people will like a photo posted on one of their Facebook friends timeline that is not professional, has no absolute value whatsoever, or is totally unnecessary. Yet, people like what is posted and do so because they are likely people who think the same as the person who posted the content, either low-minded or unaware of the unprofessionalism.

After the scandal God advised me Sam would email me, but not regarding an apology. I waited to see how many days it would take, which was about a week. Sam emailed me about upcoming events for his record label, as a promotional technique, but sent the information to my personal email instead of to our organization's entertainment division email. Although Sam emailed me about his upcoming work, he never mentioned the scandal or betrayal and never apologized (yet I sensed the email was related to the scandal and betrayal) as if he did not know *how* to apologize, but knew his acquaintance with Michelle was wrong, especially based on *my response* to the matter. Around the same time, someone emailed our entertainment division (not a subsidiary at the time) about the name on the entertainment divisions email address and why the name had changed, which was none of anyone's business, especially an anonymous email sender.

Later, someone else sent an email to my personal email address with photo attachments of Sam and I and

> "...London, and South Africa projects".

the person mentioned locating the photos online. The photos came from a private photoshoot Sam and I did with a photographer colleague of mine who later started working for our entertainment division on major print publication and media photoshoots, and hair and beauty industry trade shows for our United States, London, and South Africa projects. Only two sets of photos were printed, one for Sam and the other for me, and only two photos were shared on an old social media account of mine that no longer exists. The photoshoot was originally taken to send to a few major retailers who were working on campaigns I was considering being a part of, had changed my appearance, and needed a male in the photograph to show them what the campaign would potentially look like. Further, I rarely gave out my personal email address, so I knew someone was playing games and fishing for information and a conversation.

I played the game and commented on the photos by asking the person where did he or she retrieve the photographs from online and the photos were myself and *my best friend*. Hilariously, the person on the other end of the email messages appeared to have gotten extremely happy and responded about the best friend connation and to tried to have a conversation, which I ignored for three to four days because of work, until the person emailed me again to ask me why I was not replying. In an angry fashion I responded to tell the anonymous sender to stop contacting me or else. I believe the individual perceived I would have the capability to track him or her down and legally bring some sort of stalking or harassment case into action, so the individual never contacted me again.

On another occasion, someone emailed our entertainment division to provide praise to one of the leaders of the company, me, and what I great person I am.

After seeing the correspondence, I responded as if I was staff to see what kind of game the person would play. I advised the person on how his or her praise was accurate, other people felt the same way, Kyla has gone through a lot in life in dealing with wrongful individuals and deserved the praise, and praise should be sent to her personal email if the sender had the address. Unwittingly, the person emailed my personal email address which I switched to because I was already logged in and the person tried to send a few sentences of praise there, which I ignored.

Social Media Blocking

A few years after the scandal and betrayals I researched each person involved with the valentine's day scandal and betrayal and located their social media pages. Off and on Michelle would block and unblock her social media pages of Twitter and Instagram. For example, I believe Michelle would block her social media pages when she thought certain people were watching her actions via content she would post on her public profile. She seemed like she did not want to be scrutinized about anything, but also wanted to hide.

Case in point, I saw Michelle's name as a follower on a prominent preachers Twitter account. The prominent pastor and I know one another, and I knew about the pastor's business interests and some projects she wanted to be a part of campaign wise. After the pastor was having a conversation on social media one day with her followers, I was logged into our firm's Twitter account and "liked" one of her conversations. The pastor noticed and began sending tweets to our account to ask me if she could be added to our social media as follower, so she could get social media messages to me. Our account was blocked from any person following and restricted to business acquaintances from around the world we work with and were seeking to work with. I approved the pastor's request and she conversed with me about connecting, the process for completing an application and contract, having a meeting with me, working for our organization, and provided me with her new cell phone number.

In addition, I checked Michelle's account to see if it was open or blocked because by this time our company name was all over the pastor's social media because she was trying to get a hold of me. As I spoke with the pastor via social media and phone about a major germinal European cosmetics and hair tools company, a hair company in Atlanta, and flying to another state to work on a pastor of a mega church's project, I remembered our entities name being on her social media timeline and knew Michelle would likely see it. People check the pastors timeline very regularly. Within a small amount of time Michelle's Twitter was blocked again. The same events happened with Instagram every two to three years with the question being what or who was she hiding from, why did she continue to block *and* unblock her social media pages, and did she block them until she thought no one was no longer watching, after a couple of years?

Regarding Facebook, as I mentioned in chapter six, the account Michelle originally used to carry out the scandal against me with was deleted or deactivated and years later a new personal Facebook account for her turned up in search functions. I also reviewed Sam's social media once every few years to follow content to see and mentally document how the betrayal would play out and to secure information on the subject matter for when Sam tried to contact me in the future to have a conversation. The information would allow me to not be blind-sided, speak about the incident in error, or be in a position where I could be easily lied to and misled. I also learned from Sam's social media that he had in-person meetings with past business colleagues of mine *he met through me* which I found to be interesting and wondered how the conversation went, if the colleague asked Sam about me and what his response was.

How Deceivers Mean Business
    A colleague of mine always says, when people cannot stop you they will begin to lie on you. I found this ideation and claim to be extremely true based on the experiences I have had over the last 10 to 12 years, personally and professionally. I came to know the claim to be even more so true when a man I use to frequently minister to, pour into with encouraging words and motivation, and explain the spiritual meanings behind things he was experiencing in life and events to come mentioned in the Bible, stated the same. He warranted similar commentary when something happened to him in his personal life and since the person could not control or swindle him into something, the individual started lying on him to other people, so they would not work with his company People should not be controlling you. You should be God led/controlled and not a people pleaser (see Acts 5:29). I really encourage you to read 1 Thessalonians 2:4 where God discusses how a person who attempts to control another is trying to be God, which God has a problem with.
    The same thing happened to two other males I know. One of them works with placing celebrities on television segments for broadcasting networks, while filming inside of creative spaces, like a hard rock café. The individual who betrayed him was one of his employees,

did so with a friend of his, and afterwards the friend and his employee, in his words, "ran off to be together".

Lastly, another colleague of mine told me and a few other people one day a woman he used to counsel wanted to marry a man whom she had been with for a number of years. Eventually something happened in the relationship, she confided in her female friend, and later on down the road she found out her friend and then ex-finance were in a relationship together and engaged to be married. The female friend married the man and the woman who was wronged never heard about them ever again because she said God told her to drop the friendship and move on. A number of years later the woman found out through someone else that her ex-friend was in a physically abusive marriage with her ex-boyfriend/finance. The ex-finance was an abuser and God had spared her, but her friend went on to marry the man and had problems.

What I am trying to say is people will wear a mask and sometimes *masks*, more than one, to deceive you and wreck-havoc in your life or business. Psalm 36:2-4 is a scripture God gives me whenever I am in the presence of an evildoer. He always speaks the scripture to my spirit, particularly, about one individual to stay away from I see in public from time to time. The text reads "for he flatters *and* deceives himself in his own eyes that his iniquity will not be found out and be hated...The words of his mouth are wrong and deceitful; he has ceased to be wise *and* to do good...He plans wrongdoing on his bed; he sets himself in a way that is not good; he does not reject *or* despise evil". A lot of people plan deception, to be deliberate in their attack against you and some people do not plan deception, but become involved in it anyway. You must be careful, watchful, and discerning about both.

I have witnessed and personally experienced where people will mix deception with manipulation with the goal of controlling how a person thinks, usually when it comes to finances. When catastrophic financial events transpire in organizations, the events are not happenstance, but are usually *deliberate, planned*. People *mean* to *gain access* to your personal space or professional business to steal what they think should belong to them or to secure something they desire, using scandal, betrayal, and lying to do so.

Some persons will even have meetings with other individuals to *plan* how the catastrophe will occur, which is what God use to warn me about, traps people set. Based on personal experience, the plan is basically a trap someone sets to intentionally take you down and gain access (see Psalm 141: 9) to someone or something you have access to, with the hope of control and that you will not recover. The problem with such schemes is the wrongdoers always forget something, that God is real, does not play games, and will always right wrongs because He is holy (see Psalm 31:23; God is a God of payback). Psalm 7:16 conveys calamity will hunt a wrongdoer until the violence and mischief they planned falls on their own head.

Michelle's Christian Ministry

Matthew 25:23 explicitly states *if* you are faithful over a few things, GOD, not you, will make you ruler over many things. As an example, when you are faithful with working within someone else's business or ministry, God will give you your own. If you are dishonest or go about procuring something or someone the wrong way, complexities will result. Examples of Matthew 25:23 do not only apply to businesses or money, but are applicable to marriage, children, and the like. Treat others how you want to be treated. The latter reminds me of statements I use to hear people say when I was a child, 'do unto others as you would have them do unto you' and you will reap what you sow. Both declarations are biblical. Moreover, God works a certain way to build a ministry and heals people before appointing them to be able to help others get healed in certain areas of their lives or professions. Michelle started a ministry to blog to other women about adversities and non-adversities she faced, how she knew she needed to clean up her life, how she was raped, and more. For a while, she blogged scriptures on a website created. Approximately one month after I reviewed the website it was moved to a Facebook business fan page. The only other concern I have about the ministry is Michelle lied a lot in the past, so believing she had completely changed and blogged accurately was questionable to me, yet people can and do change.

Wheat versus Tares

When you sow positivity or a good seed you expect a good harvest. Another way to state the former is when you work hard you expect progress, growth, and greater opportunities to come to you or your organization as a result of the good work completed. The progress, growth, and greater are a part of the harvest from the good seeds sown. Yet, unfortunately, in between sowing good seeds or working hard and harvest the devil sows tares in the place where God is interested in and planning on multiplying you and your field. Tares are what God calls wolves in sheep clothing and are *pretenders* as opposed to wheat being the *real thing*. In plain English, a tare is a bad, toxic, negative person who looks, acts, and plays friendly until you recognize or directly experience their true motives, the opposite of a wheat.

Your field is what you are excellent in, your career or occupation, organization, purpose, destiny. For instance, the categories listed could be you as a hair stylist, business owner, entrepreneur, singer, author, car salesman, auto mechanic, property owner, or even an investor. Tares grow in the midst of wheat and look just like wheat, but you *can recognize* a wheat by his or her fruit, results in life. For example, tares hang around wheat, but are not wheat and are wrongdoers who think they are getting away with or have gotten away with what they have done and assume they are prospering or have prospered after a wrongdoing, but God will deal with them at the right time. God will deal with them at the time He has set if you keep quiet, watching, working, and let tares grow in *your* field, in *the* field, in the midst of wheat, side by side. Over time, as tares grow among wheat, tares typically *look* different anyway.

The purpose of not speaking on what tares have done to try to scandalize someone is to not try to deal with a negative circumstance or a foul person on your own instead of letting God do so. If you try to deal with a culprit on your own you could destroy the field your harvest or future opportunities are currently growing in and pluck up your own wheat, opportunity, or harvest too soon, when it is not time. Hence, plucking up a harvest too soon can initiate a problem with your field or next opportunity. So, keep working, silently, and let God be God while you keep communication open with God to receive directions on how God wants you to respond and what He wants you to do next, keeping your harvest safe until plucking time. On God's timing, *He will separate wheat from tare.*

God separating wheat from tare reminds of something God spoke to me about approximately one to two weeks ago. He stated He was going to deal with someone, now, who wronged me 18 years ago. She wronged me temporarily, but did damage to other people's lives permanently. The individuals who were damaged permanently were closer to and spent more time around her than I did. I advised God the only comments I had for Him were I am staying out of your way, working hard to stay out of sin, and on good terms with you.

Birthing this Book and Warning You

It takes nine months to birth a baby. The date God gave me the idea for this book was in the early hours of the morning on July 9, 2019. Prior to this, God was housing the scandal, betrayals, and lies that occurred with the individuals the book is based on within my spirit, not within my mind (will, intellect, or emotions). God housed the information in my spirit and not in my mind because He had already healed me from the incidents by taking me through a process He required me to go through to be able to continue to progress and grow spiritually and in life. God did not house this type of information in my spirit with other scandals and betrayals I encountered, only a couple, including with people from my past lying on me about various things.

Therefore, I knew God wanted me to birth something from the experiences to help others. I also knew God was greatly not pleased with the negativity that took place based on conversations we had over the years about the experiences that are the foundation of this book, who was who and who did what although they tried to hide what they did, but God would inform me, all the while I was also asking God what he wanted me to do. What He wants me to do is learn from culprits and teach and warning individuals about people's character and patterns of behaviors, to recognize the signs of scandal, betrayal, and lies, so your growth and advancement are not hindered. The same applies to your workplace or a business you may own. Be aware of schemes, character traits, or patterns of behavior people use or portray to try to commit scandal, betrayal, lies, or take advantage of you. Also, recognition and application of various personal and professional tools, instruments, and strategies can help protect a person's life, family, organization, staff, future, and legacy.

Protecting Yourself, Reputation, Career, and Ventures
Reputation is not only what you say about yourself, but regards what other people say about you. When I discussed the 98% of individuals I now interact with at the beginning of the book, I also note and keep watch of who the 98% associate with, to protect our organization and my reputation.

Not only does poor communication cause trust, rapport, and credibility issues as I outlined in chapter two, but a person's personal, team, and/or company reputation can begin to be affected, causing problems with internal and external constituents, whether they voice it or not. Principally trust issues (deriving from *poor communication skills*) within the market or industry an individual works in, with personnel of the organization, and in relationships, no matter what kind of relationships, can negatively influence key initiatives and the growth, success, and longevity of a company or a person's career.

Scandal in organizations is not limited to romance or romantic relationships, for example, or people asking leaders for money, but comes in many shapes, sizes, races, ethnicities, backgrounds, cultures, experiences, and languages. Furthermore, scandal can occur domestically and in joint ventures, alliances, loyalty agreements, personal friendships, work acquaintances, or business partnerships, via bribery, corruption, lying, deception, manipulation, fraud, embezzlement, betrayal, and the like, whether an enterprise is large or small. Being knowledgeable about and displaying trust, proper communication, rapport, credibility, and being consistently vigilant about your associations will help you protect yourself, reputation, and career.

To protect your firm or venture(s) from scandal, betrayals, and liars as must as possible, have a formal company statement of ethics, risk management, scandal management, or ethics compliance program that is regularly documented. The plan should include employees, independent contractors, non-independent contractors, and individuals who work with your organization via an established written agreement, to provide due diligence, mitigate unethical actions, and prevent reoccurrence of the misconduct. Each stakeholder or constituent of the firm should also know the company mission, vision, policies and standards, goals, and ethical priorities. Also, monitor and enforce ethical standards. Company ethical standards can be monitored and enforced using questionnaires to benchmark ongoing appraisals of conduct, consultation software, and via professional case management services, each housed in your organizations human resources department.

From each of the strategies, leaders of the firm, including you, would be required to comply with enterprise ethical standards, policies, and procedures. Further, case management software some consultants provide you can implement to protect the organization include reporting functions for worker's concerns, observations of misconduct, investigations, analysis, documentation of misconduct reports, and resolutions to be tracked and managed by complaint filed.

Besides, to protect a business, prior to hiring or working with retainers, many organizations leaders or recruiters extensively research people, usually harnessing social media. Present day social media did not exist years ago. Nevertheless, disciplinary actions to individuals who violate ethical standards, compliance, or a signed written agreement acknowledging the company's ethics rules should be developed and disseminated, and then read and understood by all members of a firm. And a company's approach to ethical standards should be modified when a method no longer works or is irrelevant.

Moreover, concerning protecting your ventures, the purpose of a business is either for shareholders or stakeholders or both. The stakeholder perspective is about leaders or managers of administrations promoting a broad range of constituent's interests, inclusive of company shareholders. Leaders or managers of a business are responsible for producing value for a variety of current sponsors or supporters of the business. The generation of value is also necessary to present the company in positive manner to future sponsors, supports, partners, and/or constituents; the reputation of the company is developed through whatever value is produced. And constituents of an organization can be either internal or external and include employees, shareholders, local communities, municipalities, and other businesses.

Overall, ensure you regularly communicate with people on your teams or successors in your personal life or professional organization who you selected to participate in certain functions, so when an outsider, lies, or lies from an outsider arises, everyone authorized to be involved with matter will be able to recognize the discrepancy or disruptor. Communication is key. In addition, affix everything in writing with the persons you selected and communicate on a regular basis about your business operations or personal affairs, so a culprit who knows each of you, but *was not selected to be a part of the team or a successor and know it* cannot come in at the last minute after a catastrophe occurs and try to lay claim to positions, power, property, or finances out of bitterness, revenge, entitlement, or greed. Each are linked with betrayal and I have seen people attempt.

Also, do not be so caught up in talking with people or working daily that you forget to settle things in writing to protect yours and organization's assets, position, and reputation. I have watched individuals nearly lose entire personal estates because they did not follow these instructions. And I know of one large organization with various subsidiaries that could have incurred major governmental fines because an important notice was not in writing so customers entering the establishment could see. This particular establishment is a large shopping mall and the issue came about because a perpetrator stated the notice was not posted and took the issue to authorities even after the organization had already checked with legal counsel on all notices that were supposed to be posted in the mall.

Wrongdoers look for loophole's in processes or between individuals where solid communication and plans are not constructed. The loophole's can either cause the downfall itself, or a downfall can be produced using the loophole in conjunction with a scandal, betrayal, lie, or all-together. So, be vigilant, perform due diligence, and double check the due diligence performed.

Blessings and Curses

Blessings and curses simply refer to if you do what God says, as a parent, being obedient to Him, you will be blessed and do well in life, if not, you will be cursed, and life will not go well for you (see Deuteronomy chapter 28). A curse is Gods recompense or pay back in someone's life and/or her or his children or future generations for sin that continued without repentance and turned into iniquity. Using *flattery in a business deal, workplace, or for a romantic relationship* to get in good with someone just to get what you want from them is unmerited and is also sin that can result in iniquity, as illustrated in Job 17:5. Job 17:5 states, "He who denounces his friends [in order to make them] a prey *and* get a share, the eyes of his children shall fail [to find food]". The scripture is powerful.

Furthermore, curses can be passed down from a person or persons down to third, fourth, and 10th generations (see Deuteronomy 23:2-5). In considering 10 generations, 10 generations are a long time which should prompt someone to understand God takes misbehavior, sin, and iniquity seriously. Too, a curse is when evil is released upon an individual to cause damage, harm, defeat, injury, destruction, drought, emotional problems, sickness or disease, mental illness, and/or *ongoing loses* of something someone values and persists in the person's life as a constant battle, adversity, spiritual war, or calamity, reducing the individual to a life of misery and causing the opposite of 3 John 2.[12]

Examples of curses are chronic sickness or disease, poverty or financial lack, female health issues, family or

---

[12] Dr. T. Williams (personal communication, August 24, 2019)

marriage problems like strife among family members or within a marriage, a history of abuse, rape, or molestation in the family bloodline, vagabondism of not be settled in life, having a stable place to live, moving from place to place, or even having to beg. Each are explained in Deuteronomy chapter 28. Henceforth, some iniquities that initiate curses are financial perversions, behavioral perversions, and perverse speech. Perversion is connected to morality and means *twisted*, a person is twisted in his or her thought processes about what is morally right versus wrong. Likewise, perversion is not always connected to sexual immorality, but primitively means a person or people are wicked, evil, corrupt, sinful, or demoralizing[13].

Financial perversions are where a person practices unjust gain, crookedness, embezzlement, misuse of money, and even dealing with illegal drugs, or abusing alcohol. Behavioral perversions derive from pride, drunkenness, unrighteous behaviors, returning evil for good, ungodly actions, abusing people, envy, sowing discord, anger, violence, verbally abusing someone, and mistreating people. Curses arising from perverse speech come from negative words, false gods, gossip, spoken curses to curse someone or his or her life, slander, profanity, crooked speech, and lying iniquities, to name a few. God specifically advised me for one of the individuals who perpetrated me during the 2008-2010 scandal, Jeremiah 20:11 would be upon the person's life. Jeremiah 20:11 states "But the Lord is with me as a mighty *and* terrible One; therefore, my persecutors will stumble, and they will

---

[13] Merriam-Webster, Inc. (2019). *Merriam-Webster dictionary app*. Retrieved from https://play.google.com/store/apps/details?id=com.merriamwebster

not overcome [me]. They will be utterly put to shame; for they will not deal wisely *or* prosper [in their schemes]; their eternal dishonor will never be forgotten".

God continuously reminds of Jeremiah 20:11. When God frequently reminds me of something, especially when the word eternal is mentioned and involves a judgement, get out of Gods way and let Him proceed, so the wrath does not come upon you, your household, or firm, causing you to receive curses instead of blessings. Knowing how God feels about dishonor, mistreating people, sin, and iniquity provokes me to be cautious about how I treat people and behave in organizations, being watchful and careful to behave ethically, morally, justly. Too, never do to others what they did to you, taking Gods place. God is in control, sees, hears, and knows everything, and will repay (see Proverbs 24:12).

Virgins Without Oil: Missed Opportunities, New Levels, and Next Dimensions of Success

Now I have fine-turned spiritual senses. What I used to tolerate and ignore for a while before dealing with or terminating from my life long after discerning adverse motives in people, I do not tolerate anymore and immediately address. Even if something unfavorable were to occur or I do not immediately address misconduct for some reason, a few of the promises God promises to do for people who believe and trust in Him are to deliver us from trouble (Psalm 91:15), affliction, adversity, and distress (Psalm 34:19), captivity (Luke 4: 18-19), evil (Matthew 6:13), fears (Psalm 34: 14), destruction (Psalm 107: 20), the will of your enemies (Psalm 41:2), every evil work (2 Timothy 4:18), temptation (2 Peter 2:9), ungodliness (Romans 11:26), and workers of iniquity and blood thirsty men (Psalm 59:1-2). Blood thirsty men are people who desire to take your life.

I discerned by God and God let me hear in the spirit, by His spirit, after researching me and finding out who I really am and some of the things I have accomplished, my adversaries had conversations about me. They likely thought I was some kind of futile, frivolous, floozy, or inconsequential individual and had conversations about it amongst one another, possibly because one person lied to the other and the person lied to was deceived, highly mistaken about me. You know, he say she say, but later discovered I am *an executive, a leader*.

Furthermore, people who are not ready for you are small people. The individuals I was involved with who are the foundation of the book, were too low for me. I was low at that time as well by dealing with them, their childish behaviors, and needed to come up higher to an executive leadership level in my thinking and shift who I deal with on a daily basis, cutting out certain people's access to me, my resources, and expertise. From a different perspective and so I do not appear boastful, some individuals are low as far as organizational level and not childish behaviors, and that is okay, but you want to carefully select who you associate with, let into your inner circle, and professional environment.

Moreover, when you see a person or people continuously going in the wrong direction in life and you frequently warn them or try to communicate the warning to them, after time passes, if they do not accept the correction let them continue on the wrong path. The best way for them to realize they went the wrong way with the wrong people or did the wrong thing is to let God reveal the misdirection and their inappropriateness to them. A prime example, although I have quite a few to share, is a man who was once a friend of mine who would not listen to me about a woman he wanted to date and when I met her I instantly began discerning things about her that were not right. God began revealing things about her to me, including an incurable sexually transmitted disease she had that existed for a little over 10 years. My friend decided to date the woman anyway, who was five to seven years older than him and came from a different upbringing.

  The concern I had with my male friend dating the woman even after I warned was he if did not believe the warning, he should have at least approached God and asked Him about the individual giving the warning (me) and about the person the warning was concerning to check into everything to be safe. Too, whenever you deal with people, whether it is the person giving the warning or the person who the warning is about, pay attention to and assess their beliefs, mind, mouth, heart, and actions to see if they align and are appropriate instead of rushing into things. Evaluate people before getting involved with them.

  The story about him did not end well. God miraculously confirmed the information for me with written and in-person documentation and told me to release the friendship with him. Not long after my friend cried for months in public at various gatherings, even when he was not trying, and everyone always wondered what was wrong. I told three people what God told me.

  Nevertheless, when dealing with people who do not listen, conduct research, and wronged you *with* culprits, the issue then becomes, God blesses the person or individuals they scandalized, betrayed, lied to or on, or wronged, *in front of them*. Betrayers will see the blessings, open doors, mega opportunities, and Glory of God bestowed, but will not partake of the blessings, missing legacy and seasons, years, decades of, and in many cases, once in a lifetime opportunities. While they were caught up in planning, carrying out, and moving on from a scandal and betrayal, you were working, abiding in light while they were moving closer and closer into darkness and unbecoming territory.

I encourage you to continue looking *and* moving forward. Scandal, betrayal, and lies are likely an indication of the people who you were acquainted with cannot handle you, are not ready for your present nor your next, and should not be a part of your long-term future. God is so wonderful, mighty, and amazing that He has a way of elevating you to new levels, even unexpected levels in life, but also to new dimensions of blessings and opportunities that are mind blowing, dimensions in life people secretly thought and privately told other people you would never achieve. If you keep moving forward without being distracted by the scandals, betrayals, and lies, God will show you that He can make a fool out of fools as I stated before. Some fools are even on talking terms with God, but that does not mean God favors them and is pleased with their ways. God will speak with them when they ask Him questions, but will advise you, the faithful one, the non-betrayer, of something different, how to recover, what will happen to them, and how to accomplish your dreams, providing *you* with more details on how to succeed in life.

Restoration of Everything, and then Some

When everything is said and done, and God fights your battles, you will come out with the victory and still be standing, sometimes the last one standing while perpetrator's organizations, associations, and progress have dissolved. Or as my Pastor says, culprits continuously try to start *different* ventures, sometimes disguised as being for God, but not ever really get anything off the ground or are successful, blooming were planted. And keep this in mind, sin only lasts for a season (Hebrews 11:25) and when you forgive others God will forgive you, but also when you forgive others, God will restore you (see Job 42:10).

    Although the valentine's day scandal and betrayal along with all of the events that occurred afterwards, I found out that God was working on my behalf, preparing a feast for me and my life, a table before me in the very presence of my enemies (see Psalm 23:5) to receive the opportunity to birth this book and more. I highly recommend you read 1 Corinthians 2:9. Everything I went through, God allowed, to fit into His master plan to get me into places, spaces, and opportunities He pre-destined for my life.

    Conclusively, God will redeem friendships, time, and money spent, wasted, and/or stolen with seven-year, 21-year, or 30, 60, 90-fold retributions. Recompense does not come back the same way it left, but bigger, better, and greater. Remember, God is an adder and multiplier and loves multiplying, hence, the tithes and offering concept I explained to you at the close of chapter three in the scripture references section. Scandals, betrayals, liars, trials, or troubles will come and are a part of life, but God will ensure the same people who watched or tried to take you down, watch you go up. Many will be disgusted at the fact that they have to watch you succeed, will wish they never wronged you, and God will get all of the glory for the process. Take care for now.

SCRIPTURE REFERENCES

Biblical scriptures always help to put people, places, and things into perspective. Following, are scripture references, red flags, and lessons I learned as I reflected on what took place with people I dealt with in chapter seven:

- In considering how deceivers mean business and possessing knowledge about how wheat differ from tares, Isaiah 54:17 expounds, "Not one weapon formed against you will prosper and every tongue or mouth that rises against you in judgement, God will *prove* to be wrong".
- Always remember to forgive others because when you need to be forgiven you will receive forgiveness. Luke 6:37 postulates, "...acquit *and* forgive *and* release (give up resentment, let it drop), and you will be acquitted *and* forgiven *and* released".
- As I remember how God told me to release friendships or associations with various people, I did. Amos 3:3 clarifies extremely well what God was having me do by explicating, "How can two walk together except they agree"? The scripture is true. And I am referring to constructive or healthy agreements and disagreements, not situations where you constantly have problems with people or God warns you connections with individuals will be very problematic later. I have had *deep experience* in this area with people and know what God is referencing, so cut ties with people when necessary instead of letting the association drag on.
- Regarding not being associated with individuals where constant disagreement occurs and the disagreement is not constructive disagreement or criticism, it is very critical for you to not be unequally yoked with

unbelievers or people who practice iniquity, unrighteousness, wrongdoing, lawless, immorality, or unhealthy relationships when you practice righteousness and seek godly, appropriate, faithful, loyal, respectful, sincere, enduring, and trustworthy connections. Second Corinthians 6:14-18 illustrates light cannot have fellowship with darkness. Unequally yoked means connected to, in business with, or acquainted with and unbelievers is not limited to religion. Unbelievers can be people who are not headed in the same direction in life as you, business colleagues or organizations who do not share similar interests and would be detrimental to an aspect of your firm, or individuals who do not share your vision or support your efforts, but want you to do so for them.

- To practice waiting on God and His timing (so you do not acquire undesirable results) after you asked God what He wants you to do about a negative situation: Psalm 62:1-2 contends, "For God alone my soul waits in silence; from Him comes my salvation. He only is my Rock and my Salvation, my Defense *and* my Fortress, I shall not be greatly moved". Remember, only consider the observation route if God tells you to. If He advises you to He has a purpose for it.
- While waiting on God and His timing after you asked God what He wants you to do about a negative situation, Psalm 31:14-15 states, "But I trusted in, relied on, *and* was confident in You, O Lord; I said, You are my God. My times are in Your hands; deliver me from the hands of my foes and those who pursue me *and* persecute me". Foes are enemies and enemies are people who are opposed to you succeeding in life or at something. You need to know who such people are and have a strategy from God on how to handle them

while you still advance because they *will* attempt to stop you, whether through scandals, betrayals, lies, or traps.
- Even if you fall into a scandal, betrayal, lie, or trap, Psalm 34:19 elucidates, "Many evils confront the [consistently] righteous, but the Lord delivers him out of them all". God did not say He would deliver or free you from one scandal, betrayal, lie, or trap, but all of them. In addition, Deuteronomy 28:7 explains, The Lord will cause people or enemies you rise up against you one way to flee before you seven ways. People *will not* get away with what they have done to you or an organization. God *is* in control.
- Inclusive, if you are scandalized, betrayed, or lied on, Proverbs 6:31 claims, "…But if he is found out, he must restore seven times [what he stole], he must give the whole substance of his house [if necessary – to meet his fine]". Essentially, whenever you catch a thief stealing, he *must* repay seven-fold of what he stole. This is the seven-year recompense I conveyed earlier in the text. However, go to God about this because sometimes God will grant you double or triple the amount of time, finances, belongings, or other compensation (with accrued interest) depending on the type of incident that occurred and how much time has passed. Remember, God is an added and multiplier.
- And after God releases a judgement on your adversaries and informs you, keep Proverbs 24:17-20 in mind so you do not lose any recompense God rewarded you or that is on the way. The scripture explicates, "Rejoice not when your enemy falls, and let not your heart be glad when he stumbles *or* is overthrown. Lest the Lord see it and it be evil in His eyes *and* displease Him, and He turn away His wrath

from Him [to expend it upon you, the worse offender]. Fret not because of evildoers, neither be envious of the wicked. For there shall be no reward for the evil man; the lamp of the wicked shall be put out".
- After a scandal or betrayal against you, conceptualized using falsehood, there shall be glory. This means the same as God will reward, recompense, and pay you for your suffering. God has numerous ways of compensating people who were scandalized, betrayed, or lied on, some natural compensation and some of the compensation will be given in eternity, details beyond the scope of this text. Yet, God will be gloried when the scandals and betrayals are finished because perpetrators will recognize God was in the situation and was and still is with *you* and not a dirty scheme. First Peter 5:10 explains this as, "And after you have suffered a little while, the God of all grace [Who imparts all blessing and favor], Who has called you to His [own] eternal glory in Christ *Jesus*, will Himself complete *and* make you what you ought to be, established *and* ground you securely, and strengthen, and settle you". Completing you and making you what you ought to be is restoration; Romans 8:28 implies all things, whether good or bad, are working together on your behalf, for your good, in your favor.

RED FLAGS
- If you are involved with any deceitful encounters conveyed in this book, get out of them as quickly as you can. God does release judgement upon individuals who practice sin and do not repent. To repent means to have a change of mind, heart, and action towards something or someone and go in the

opposite direction of what you previously thought or did, a new direction.
- If you are or were a victim of similar scandals, betrayals, or deceitfulness discussed in the book, forgive people who wrongfully pursued you, repent if you have not forgiven, and go in a different direction. Unforgiveness opens a door in your life spiritually for other sins to enter, later curses, and following iniquity and generational issues for individuals born after you, for example, your children.

LESSONS LEARNED
- If you do not forgive people who hurt, wronged, or offended you, God cannot forgive you of your trespasses; quickly forgive people for their wrongdoing, in general, and to avoid stagnation in your natural life and spiritually. Mark 11:26 contends, "But if you do not forgive, neither will your Father in heaven forgive your failings and shortcomings".
- Individuals will pretend like they do not remember their sins against you by attempting to speak with you again about something not related to their sins against you without acknowledging what they wrongfully did to you, like you forgot. Acknowledgement of what they did to you before conversating with you or asking you for something should be the first statement out of the person's mouth.
- Wait for God and His strategies to vindicate, reward, redeem, fight for, and exalt you, *exposing* false people, scandals, betrayers, and liars. The same scandal, betrayal, wrongdoing, and dirt meant to remove, stop, hurt, and bury me *raised me*. Also, never let hurt, pain, situations, or people dominate you, your emotions, or

feelings, ultimately directing your life, advancement, and accomplishments.
- I will tell you what I tell people when I minister to them at church or speak to them outside of church about a situation, as a leader, never let devils, circumstances, people, rejection, or life *wipe you out* or take you out. *Never let a devil outlast you.* Always get back up after being knocked down. And get God involved in every battle or war, so victory is *guaranteed*. I am very adamite about not letting people or circumstances wipe me out or let the devil outlast me when God has too much power, has given me power, and both of us together have much more power than an enemy.
- God will provide you with a strategy to recover *everything*, finances, time, resources, and efforts spent or wasted on other people or God will supernaturally shift whatever you lost or what was deliberately stolen from you back into your possession (see 1 Samuel 30:8). I have experienced so.

CHAPTER KEY POINTS

- How you respond to scandal, betrayers, liars, and inquiring with and waiting on God to avenge reveals your level of maturity or immaturity and character.
- You can miss God or your next level or dimension of success by following or listening to people God did not tell you to listen to or follow (see Psalms chapter 1). Be *very* careful of who you let speak into your life, whether family members, friends, associates, or business acquaintances. Matthew 24:4 (AMP) warrants, "Jesus answered them, Be careful that no one misleads you [deceiving you and leading you into error]. Similarly, never follow a person who has no oil.

You can read about the 'foolish virgin's' in the Bible who missed God because they did not have any oil in their lamps in Matthew 25:1-13. Mainly the text illustrates, if people who live in a city know a storm is coming in two days, foolish people might attend parties and engage in drinking while instead of partying, non-foolish (wise) people gather gasoline for vehicles before gas stations run out of fuel, call relatives in a different city or state to make plans to live with them until the storm passes, gather food, batteries, and first aid kits, secure their homes and businesses, prepare their children and clothing, and ensure pets are well fed and ready.

- Additionally, one hour before the storm is expected, foolish people who wake up from sleeping after a night of partying and drinking begin to see people getting on the interstate to leave town will approach neighbors to ask if they have any *extra* food, supplies, or gasoline, but God will prompt them to reply, you should have prepared when it was time to prepare instead of following worthless, insignificant, valueless pursuits. Put another way, you should have been working, building a business, growing in God, learning strategies, and investing in yourself instead of scandalizing, betraying, lying, jet skiing, taking personal vacations, and spending time with individuals who are not connected to your *next*. In urban communities, individuals call this, 'you should have been making moves'. If anything, travel for business or purpose and after meetings take one hour for personal time to enjoy the city you traveled to. Yet, the virgin's without oil scripture and story is what God advised me is *presently* happening to my betrayers, so I had to include the story in the book.

- Be careful not to interfere with the plans and purposes God has for someone's life or organization. Interference will *cost* you, usually when you are unaware. Discipline or judgement from God can be spiritual with natural manifestations, in the form of curses I discussed with you earlier. Poverty and financial lack are a frequent judgement I see people go through.

A QUICK PRAYER

- An avenue to experience victory over evil, an enemy, a perpetrator (*traitor*), or simply someone who did you wrong is to:
    1. Forgive every person who wrong you (Mark 11:25).
    2. Renounce and repent of all of your own sins (Acts 20:21)
    3. Speak Gods word against who or what is going coming after you (Mark 11:23-24).
    4. Complete steps one through three with a quick prayer. I created one for you below.
- Here is a quick prayer I developed for you to pray a loud to God in the comfort of your own home or to whisper to God where ever you are, to identify your pain, tell God, be open to His advice and strategies, forgive scandalous people, betrayers, and liars, and to get free, clearing the way in your behaviors, attitude, heart, and mind (will, intellect, and emotions), so God can continue to bless, advance, and promote you in life. The prayer will free you from being bound by the trick of operating in self-led revenge or *evil worthless fruit*.
- We begin with you giving your life to Jesus Christ (God) to be your Lord and Savior, which is a prerequisite to receiving Gods divine assistance. Lord means God is the leader of your life, providing you

with guidance, direction, and strategies to navigate life, business, and circumstances, and Savior means you need to be saved or rescued from something, like hell, enemies, threatening letters, betrayers, sickness, curses, bad business deals, and so on:

> *Dear God,*
> *I am a sinner, have been hurt by someone, or hurt someone through scandal, betrayal, or lying and need a Savior. Help me. I repent of any wrongdoing I did to others, forgive people who wronged me, and I believe in my heart and confess with my mouth Jesus bled and died on the cross for my mistakes and You raised (**rose**) Him from the dead to save me. Jesus, come into my heart and make me the person You want me to be. I cover my faults and the faults others did to me with the blood of Jesus and release evildoers from me, self-led revenge, and the production of evil worthless fruit in my life, business, or relationships. God, thank you for new doors, new opportunities, new connections, new contracts, and a new me no one can stop.*
> In Jesus' Name I pray, Amen.

AUTHOR BIOGRAPHY

Dr. Kyla Latrice Tennin (preferably Dr. K) is a transformational leader with *core values* of compassion (positivity), leadership, dependability, equality (fairness), and determination, and has executive education experience at Harvard and Stanford Universities, has been an entrepreneur for nearly two decades, and has successfully launched numerous corporations within 26 locations, in 24 countries, on 6 continents. Most of Dr. K's international experience (e.g. leadership, management, advisory services, consulting, negotiations, human resources, etc.) has been virtual, so her interest in ground experience is high. Further, Dr. K is known for being detailed, operates in integrity and excellence, and follows a *personal mission statement* of "to use my gift of leadership to serve as a determined and dependable leader who shows equality and compassion to others around the world, especially women and girls".

Also, Dr. K is a recipient of over 30 organizational awards, has over 20 years of experience in her industry, and *15 years* of experience leading her own *global conglomerate* firm as President and Global CEO, with early beginnings in 1998. Her work spans working with Fortune 500, 100 and 1000 companies as the firm's global corporate clients, such as: Procter & Gamble, Macy's, L'Oréal International, Belk department stores, Kmart, and foreign governments, and registered diverse supplier for corporations like Coty, Inc., Kohl's, Nordstrom department stores, Johnson and Johnson, The Limited Brands, The Coca-Cola Company, airlines and airports, municipalities in distinguished nations, and so on.

Additionally, Dr. K has a high interest in consumer product development of natural/green/organic products, particularly cosmeceuticals and nutricosmetics (topical and oral agents) appearance-related product categories using natural sciences, botanicals, spices, and food (e.g. vitamins). Her *value proposition* is deep expertise in *organizational infrastructure and business administration-executive office to solve business architecture and administration complexities* with an objective of resurrecting financial and operational output to accomplish profitable and sustainable growth.

Further, Dr. K holds a social sciences *practitioner doctorate of Doctor of Management in Organizational Leadership (DM)* from the University of Phoenix College of Doctoral Studies, formerly the School of Advanced Studies. She has non-profit management studies and Doctor of Philosophy (PhD) *research doctorate* credits from Capella University in Minneapolis, Minnesota in Non-profit Leadership with a concentration on Boards, CEO's, and Board Governance, a Master's in Business Administration (MBA) from the University of Phoenix in Minneapolis, Minnesota, a Bachelor of Arts (BA) in Women's Studies with minors in Biology (Pre-Medicine Studies) and Conflict Resolution Studies from private institution Hamline University in St. Paul, Minnesota. Too, she has knowledge and professional experience in global intellectual property, reputational issues, various corporate environments and cultures, leadership, sales, organizational diagnosis, intervention, and implementation, research, banking, regulations, credit, strategy, assessments, and marketing.

Prior to launching her own main enterprise, Dr. K worked in operations and finance at SunTrust Banks, Inc., US Bank, and Wells Fargo Bank, N.A. with affiliate global relationships with Wells Fargo Financial, Wells Fargo Auto Finance, Wells Fargo Card Services, Wells Fargo Business

Banking, Wells Fargo Investments, Wells Fargo Education, and Wells Fargo Home Mortgage. As an exemplar, she assisted with the launch of Wells Fargo Bank locations in fourteen southern states (M&A)), was a *high-performer, top sales employee, received various awards, and scored over 95%, consistently, on quality assurance.* As a fun fact, did you know there is a Wells Fargo Bank ATM located on the *North Pole* at McMurdo Station, operated by the locals? Equally, in the very early days of Dr. K's career, she serviced and operated ATM machines, digitally, nationwide in the USA, for US Bank Corporation.

Dr. K continues practitioner scholarship at global conferences and has worked with Board of Directors in two private, one public, and four nonprofit corporations. Meanwhile being registered to serve on boards of directors and advisory boards for public and private corporations in Europe, the Middle East, and Africa (EMEA), Asia, Japan, North America (the United States of America and Canada), and Latin America.

Moreover, with proven experience and national awards, Dr. K has volunteered with over 20 organizations and participated in as a speaker and assisted with creating leadership conferences, workshops, entrepreneur and career symposium panels, mentoring and coaching at the University of Phoenix to teach current students and alumni about starting a business (whether for-profit or non-profit), writing a business plan, investor pitches, venture capital, foreign entities, business proposals, and grant writing. Dr. K has also served on several Boards of Directors to *conceptualize committees, approve budgets, and establish objectives and policies, and is a member of nine investment firms,* reviewing business plans, project financials, and pitches for start-up enterprises regularly. She currently writes business, management, leadership, and entrepreneurship curriculum on a project and consulting basis for Western Governor's University under the corporation Ms. Kyla Latrice, Inc.

Finally, Dr. K's leadership and entrepreneurship focuses are global and specific, as she also possesses cross-functional experience and *deep expertise in operations and strategy as a global leader.* Likewise, she has written 14 books, over *80 research reports (inclusive of presentations)* about enterprises, and participated in a peer-reviewed published empirical research *Fulbright* Scholarship Tanzania Africa Molecular Biology and Bio-Technology project available here:
http://onlinelibrary.wiley.com/doi/10.1002/bmb.2004.49 4032060401/full#.UkxJd9NAUd4.twitter

For co-author, editorial, and corporation, association, university, or faith-based speaker requests, contact: Lady Mirage Agency, Inc. via:
www.LadyMirageGlobal.com

www.ingramcontent.com/pod-product-compliance
Lightning Source LLC
Chambersburg PA
CBHW071231080526
44587CB00013BA/1562